ENDORSEMENTS

God is making a distinction between believers and the world. No matter what happens to the world, if you are not a "stranger to the covenant," you will walk under an open heaven and supernatural favor. This is a biblical "how to" book, that *will* make a difference!

SID ROTH, Author
Host, *It's Supernatural!* television program

You hold in your hands a treasure beautifully penned by Pastor Kynan. He has done an amazing job in capturing the Lord's heart concerning divine favor. There are truths and revelations written here that will bring your life into new dimensions of the Lord's blessings. I highly recommend this book as it will take you into the set time of favor, and I encourage you to share these anointed insights with others as well. It's time for *Supernatural Favor!*

HANK KUNNEMAN
Senior Pastor, Lord of Hosts Church, Omaha, Nebraska
Founder and President of One Voice Ministries

The description of the heavens in Genesis 1 prior to being named was "the expanse." It actually means "the expander" or "the expanding thing." Hebrew scholars tell us that the word means "the arranger" or "the placer." Heaven is the expansive and ever-expanding covering over us from which all things are arranged and placed in our lives by a loving Father, The Father of Lights, who gives good gifts to His children, and in whom there is no shadow of turning. His faithfulness reaches to the heavens, and He surrounds us with favor as with a shield. Pastor Kynan Bridges invites us in his newest work to live under an open heaven and gain a heavenly perspective of the endless ever-expanding possibilities available to us because of God's goodness. Take your time as you read through *Supernatural Favor* and enjoy the rich insights he offers for a life lived in and for God's highest and best.

Dr. Mark J. Chironna
Church on the Living Edge
Mark Chironna Ministries

The favor of God is truly one of the most profound blessings God bestows on a person. When we seek God's face, not His hands, we gain the understanding that a relationship with God means a daily, intimate, loving pursuit of the desires of God's heart. When friendship with God is our constant obsession, favor is the supernatural by-product that manifests in our lives. Pastor Bridges's new book *Supernatural Favor—Living in God's Abundant Supply* will give you the vital keys to transform your mind in order to receive the favor of God in every area of your life by tapping into the abundance of God's overflowing goodness and grace.

Dr. Barbie L. Breathitt, Ph.D.
Author, *Dream Encounters—Seeing Your Destiny from God's Perspective*,
and *Gateway to the Seer Realm—Look Again to See Beyond the Natural*

Supernatural
FAVOR

DESTINY IMAGE BOOKS BY KYNAN BRIDGES

Possessing Your Healing

Supernatural
FAVOR

Living in God's **ABUNDANT** Supply

Kynan Bridges

DESTINY IMAGE® PUBLISHERS, INC.

P.O. Box 310, Shippensburg, PA 17257-0310

"Promoting Inspired Lives."

This book and all other Destiny Image, Revival Press, MercyPlace, Fresh Bread, Destiny Image Fiction, and Treasure House books are available at Christian bookstores and distributors worldwide.

For a U.S. bookstore nearest you, call 1-800-722-6774.

For more information on foreign distributors, call 717-532-3040.

Reach us on the Internet: www.destinyimage.com.

ISBN 13 TP: 978-0-7684-4240-3

ISBN 13 Ebook: 978-0-7684-8465-6

For Worldwide Distribution, Printed in the U.S.A.

2 3 4 5 6 7 8 / 17 16 15 14

DEDICATION

This book is dedicated to the Lord Jesus Christ; the Source through whom all power and blessings flow. To my lovely wife, Gloria; a virtuous woman who has continued to support and inspire me every day. To my children; you drive me to excellence. To my spiritual children and church family; God bless you, and thank you for supporting this book.

CONTENTS

Preface 11

1   The Blessing of Abraham 13

2   The Favor Factor 21

3   An Open Heaven 31

4   All Grace Abounds 43

5   Favor as Our Birthright 53

6   Faith and Favor 65

7   Financial Favor 77

8   Unlimited Favor 91

9   On the Edge of the Blessing 103

10 Soul Prosperity 115

11 Thinking Differently 125

12 It's Already Yours 135

13 No More Lack 143

14 An Abundant Supply 155

15 Living in the Overflow 165

PREFACE

ALL OF MY LIFE, I WAS TOLD THAT I WAS DIFFERENT FROM EVERY-one around me. I spoke differently, walked differently, and even thought differently from those in my environment. This became even more evident when I became born again in the early 1990s. Through-out my Christian journey, I discovered what set me apart from my peers—the favor of God. In my studies of Abraham, the great father of our faith, I came across an ancient biblical secret to living in a dimension of the tangible goodness of God every day of our lives. I found the answers to what set Abraham apart from the people of his day, what caused Abraham to walk in spiritual, physical, and emotional prosperity his entire life, and discovered that it is possible for Christians today to live in that same abundance.

How are Christians to move in these trying economic times? I believe that the Word of God promises every born-again believer the same favor that was on Abraham!

Chapter 1

THE BLESSING OF ABRAHAM

*That the blessing of Abraham might come
on the Gentiles through Jesus Christ;
that we might receive the promise of the
Spirit through faith* (Galatians 3:14).

ONE OF MY FAVORITE SUNDAY SCHOOL HYMNS WAS A SONG
called "Father Abraham." The lyrics of the song said, "Father
Abraham, had many sons. Many sons had father Abraham. I am one
of them and so are you, so let's just praise the Lord." I must have

sung this song a million times. There was something so profound about this song that I could never fully wrap my mind around. This song always made me happy every time I sung it, but it always left me with internal questions.

The reality was, I did not really have a clue what I was singing. What does it mean to be a seed of Abraham? How can a person who died thousands of years ago have any relation to me, and what does this relationship imply? Like most of my peers, I did not dare ask questions about this in public. Besides, we were just children; it probably did not matter what we were singing anyway, right? Wrong! I later discovered that this song had more significance than I could have even imagined.

I believe that the lyrics to that song, as well as my questions about them, holds the key to releasing the supernatural favor of God in the lives of everyday believers. I believe that the answer to the question, "What does it mean to be a seed of Abraham?" is a secret to living in God's abundant supply. In fact, the answer to this question is so powerful that it has radically reshaped my life as a Christian and it has the divine potential to radically reshape your life as well.

In the book of Galatians, the Bible tells us that the blessing of Abraham has come on the Gentiles by faith. What does this mean? Well before we can answer that question, we must first learn more about Abraham. Abraham is the father of our faith. He is the father of the Jewish people. In Genesis 12:1, God called Abram (later renamed Abraham) and his family out of his country and away from his kins-men, and told him to go to a land that He (God) would show him. Can you imagine how frightening something like this must have been? Can you imagine leaving all that you know and are familiar with behind? Well, that is exactly what God told Abraham to do, and this required a ridiculous amount of faith to accomplish. In fact, God made a promise with Abraham in the next two verses; Genesis 12:2-3 says:

> *And I will make of thee a great nation, and I will bless thee, and make thy name great; and thou shalt be a blessing: And I will bless them that bless thee, and curse him that curseth thee:* **and in thee shall all families of the earth be blessed.**

God actually told Abraham that He would not only bless him, but in him would *all* the families of the earth be blessed. This is pretty amazing! The first thing that God did after He called Abraham out of his country was make a promise to him. God never breaks His promise! When God spoke this promise to Abraham, there was something that immediately transferred to him in the spiritual realm. Abraham became a blessed man! The Hebrew word for blessed is the word *barak* (Strong's, H1288). This word literally means to bless or to cause to kneel. This blessing on Abraham's life would cause situations, circumstances, finances, people, and even nations to kneel before him. He was magnetized with the supernatural favor of God. In fact, Genesis 13:2 says that Abram was very rich in cattle, in silver, and in gold.

> *This blessing on Abraham's life would cause situations, circumstances, finances, people, and even nations to kneel before him.*

Why was Abraham experiencing this newfound material success? It was the power of the blessing that God spoke over his life. He was blessed, and who God blesses, no one can curse. In the 14th chapter of Genesis, Abraham engages in the slaughter of the kings (see Genesis 14:17) and meets a very interesting person named Melchizedek (which I believe to be Christ revealed in the Old Testament). This Melchizedek was a priest of the Most High God and the king of Salem. This king of Salem blessed Abram and said: "Blessed be Abram of the most high God, possessor of heaven and earth: And blessed be the most high God, which hath delivered thine enemies into thy hand. And he gave him tithes of all" (Genesis 14:19-20). So we see consistently, that everywhere Abraham went he was blessed by both God and man. Abraham walked in supernatural favor!

THE FATHER OF MANY NATIONS

Finally, in Genesis 15:6, Abraham believes in the promise that God gave him of having a son spring forth from his own loins and he believes in the Lord and it was "counted to him for righteousness." In Genesis 17, God changes Abram's name to Abraham because he is to be the "father of many nations." God promises Abraham an innumerable amount of physical and spiritual children as a result of their covenant relationship. Then God gave Abraham the symbol of circumcision to ratify this covenant. Through Abraham, every nation on the earth will be blessed. This is a promise so momentous that it could not even be actualized in Abraham's lifetime.

This is the blessing that Paul is referring to in Galatians 3:14. As a matter of fact, the Bible tells us that Christ is the seed of Abraham spoken of in Genesis 13:15. Simply put, we have received this blessing that was on Abraham's life through the shed blood of Jesus Christ. Through Jesus, Gentile believers have been granted access to the original covenant that God made with Abraham and to the nation of Israel. Though God's original covenant with His people, Israel still stands, the Gentiles have been grafted into this covenant through the body of Christ. As a matter of fact, we have received an even better covenant in the body of Messiah Jesus. We, like the physical descendants of Abraham, are the seed of Abraham.

When I was a 6-year-old singing that lovely song in church, I was actually proclaiming the supernatural favor and blessing of God over my own life and didn't even realize it. In the Abrahamic covenant was an ancient mystery that could unlock favor, blessings, and prosperity in the life of every born-again believer. Many Christians do not know what it means to be blessed in Abraham. We don't comprehend the full ramifications of not only being heirs of righteousness by faith, but also being heirs of the favor of God. There is a supernatural favor available to us that has the power to change our lives forever. A revelation of God's divine favor has been one of the greatest things that has ever happened to my family, ministry, and finances.

WHAT IS FAVOR?

We have already examined several examples of supernatural favor. We have seen the demonstrations of supernatural favor in the life of the father of our faith: Abraham. It may do us well to define favor. What is favor? Webster's Dictionary defines favor as an attitude of approval or liking; to give unfairly preferential treatment to. This is very interesting! In fact, favor is when you and I are preferred or liked. The Hebrew word for favor is *chen* (Strong's, H2580) and it means favor, grace, and charm.

So what do we mean by the term supernatural favor? When we use the term supernatural favor, we are referring to a supernatural state of preferential treatment and an attitude of acceptance that God demonstrates toward us. Abraham was blessed by God and this blessing attracted favor from both God and man. This favor caused a positive reaction in every area of Abraham's life. The good news is that you and I have access to this favor in even greater measure through Jesus Christ our Lord.

The problem that most Christians have is that, like me for many years, they are unaware of this favor. We are not accidents going somewhere to happen. We are blessings going somewhere to happen! There is a realm of existence that is much higher than the mundane rat race of life. We have not been called by God to struggle and strive to simply survive, but we have been given the legal right in Christ to thrive. God wants us to walk in a level of victory that we may not have experienced up to this point. I am here to tell you that there is so much more available to us.

> *We are not accidents going somewhere to happen.*
> *We are blessings going somewhere to happen!*

How would you like to be on the right side of heaven? How would you like to have the favor of God activated in your home, ministry, finances, and your physical body? What if there was a place in God of supernatural advantage that could catapult you far beyond where you are right now? Well, there is a place, and it is called the favor of God!

FAVOR DECLARATION

Father, in the name of Jesus Christ, I thank You for who You are and all that You have done in my life. I thank You that I am a seed of Abraham and that the blessing of Abraham has come on me through Jesus Christ. Just as Abraham walked in Your supernatural favor; I walk in Your favor in every area of my life. I declare that I have victory over the circumstances of my life and that I am blessed of the Most High. In Jesus' name. Amen!

Chapter 2

THE FAVOR FACTOR

*And Joseph's master took him, and put him into
the prison, a place where the king's prisoners
were bound: and he was there in the prison. **But
the LORD was with Joseph, and shewed him
mercy, and gave him favour in the sight of
the keeper of the prison*** (Genesis 39:20-21).

GROWING UP IN A SPIRIT-FILLED CHURCH ENVIRONMENT, I
often heard the phrase "Favor Isn't Fair!" Usually this meant
that someone had received some sort of promotion or blessing that
they did not deserve. In other words, it was unmerited. The promotion,

money, or other blessing was not based on education or job performance, but it was based solely on God's favorable attitude toward the person on the receiving end. This is what I call the "Favor Factor."

What do I mean by the term Favor Factor? I am speaking of being in the flow of God's favor. I am talking about strategically placing ourselves in a position where we are aligned with heaven's blessings. It is a place where God is smiling on you. We see this favor factor demonstrated in Joseph's life.

Joseph was a descendant of Abraham. The same favor that was on Abraham's life was on Joseph's life as well. Joseph operated in such a powerful dimension of the favor of God that even while he was in prison, he received preferential treatment. The Bible says in Genesis 39 that when the master took him and put him into prison, after being falsely accused by Potiphar's wife, that God was with him and gave him *favor* in the sight of the keeper of the prison. This is an awesome display of the impact of the favor of God on our lives. We can experience this favor even in the worst of physical circumstances.

When I was younger, I loved to watch Michael Jordan play basketball. Jordan may very well go down in history as the greatest basketball player of all time. When I would watch him play, I was fascinated by how long he could stay in the air. It was as if he glided through the atmosphere every time he went to dunk the basketball into the hoop. Some would say that he played gracefully. There was something about the way he played basketball that set him apart from the rest of the players. There was an uncanny ability that he possessed on the court.

This is what I am referring to when I speak of the favor factor, it is an advantage that we possess that separates us from the crowd. Joseph possessed this advantage. He was looked at differently from his peers. As Joseph worked within the prison system of his day, he was given greater stewardship responsibility than the other prisoners. In fact, he eventually became the head of the prison. Isn't that wonderful? The Favor Factor that I am referring to is not a natural favor that we saw demonstrated in a personality like Michael Jordan—this is a supernatural advantage that we possess as a result of our relationship with God through Jesus Christ. This supernatural favor on our lives can open doors that no one can close. Later we will examine in more detail the New Covenant paradigm of God's divine favor, but for now I want to share some encounters with this supernatural favor that have reshaped our lives.

> *This supernatural favor on our lives can open doors that no one can close.*

BLESSED AND HIGHLY FAVORED

And the angel came in unto her, and said, Hail, thou that art highly favoured, the Lord is with thee: blessed art thou among women (Luke 1:28).

Several years ago my wife went to a woman's conference. At this time we were not in full-time ministry. Toward the end of the conference, the facilitator opened up the session for prayer. My wife told me that as she was praying, she saw a circle in the spirit realm. It was like a circle of supernatural light. She heard the voice of the Lord speak to her and tell her to "step in." As she stepped into the circle, she experienced a supernatural manifestation of the anointing of God on her life like never before. She wept in this wonderful presence. When my wife came home from that conference, she was a different person. She was more bold, more confident, and more efficient in ministering to other women.

What happened in that moment? I believe that the favor of God was activated on her life. It was always present, but it needed to be activated and released. She began to take advantage of the Favor Factor. As she stepped into that circle, she was stepping into a place of power, ability, and anointing. This is what the Favor Factor is all about. It is a place where we are no longer depending on ourselves, but we are depending on God's power.

In the New Testament, the favor of God is not just manifested as preferential treatment, but as grace. In fact the word favor is translated many times as grace. What is meant by the term grace? In every appearance of the word grace in the New Testament, it is translated from the Greek word *charis*. This Greek word is something that scholars are still trying to wrap their minds around. Most often it is used to express the idea of unmerited favor, but it also means supernatural power and ability. The grace or favor of God grants us a supernatural endowment to accomplish the purpose and plan of God for our lives. This favor accelerates, transforms, and renews us. Like my wife, we need to step into this supernatural reality. Can you imagine what it would be like if you began to live life from the position of God's power and not your own? Can you imagine the level of relief that you will experience once you no longer rely on your ability? This is what it means to be "blessed and highly favored."

> *The grace or favor of God grants us a*
> *supernatural endowment to accomplish the*
> *purpose and plan of God for our lives.*

IN THE SIGHT OF GOD AND MAN

And Jesus increased in wisdom and stature, and in favour
with God and man (Luke 2:52).

In the natural realm, people only respond to what they can see with their eyes and perceive with their senses. For example, employees usually have an annual performance review. This performance evaluation is based on the employee accomplishing specific tasks and reaching predetermined milestones. The manager observes the employee's behavior to see if the milestones were reached. If he didn't see any progress in the natural, he cannot promote the employee. Everything in this world system is driven by what we see.

When I was in the corporate world, I often heard the slogan, "Perception is reality." This means that the way people perceive you has the power to determine how they treat you. If an employee is perceived as lazy and counterproductive, then the person is usually not considered for raises and career advancement. The fatal flaw with this system is the limitation of visibility. An employee may do a wonderful job, but if the person is not *seen* doing the wonderful job then he or she may not be externally rewarded.

The favor of God has the supernatural ability to increase our visibility when and where it counts. This is what the Bible means when it says "favor in the sight of God and man." Why is this so important?

The Bible says in Luke 6:38, "Give and it shall be given unto you; good measure, pressed down, and shaken together, and running over, shall men give into your bosom." Notice that God uses men to give into our bosom. This doesn't mean that God always uses a person, but it does mean that some people have been ordained as instruments in God's hand to bless us. The favor of God has the power to cause men and women to see you. When the favor of God is operating in your life, it will draw the attention of godly helpers and promoters.

To give you an example of the favor of God working in this way, I will share with you a story. Several years ago, my wife and children and I went out to evangelize with a large church in our area. Once we got to where we were to share the Gospel, we began to talk to all sorts of people. At one point we came upon a group of young people who were smoking marijuana. As the leader began to open her mouth to speak to the young people, they dismissed her and mocked her. I thought it would be a good idea if I stepped in. I began to share with the young people God's love for them; and as I did, an amazing thing happened—they put out their joints and removed their hats. They began to listen to every word I said. Afterward, they said the prayer of salvation; all eight of them! Hallelujah!

After we were finished witnessing, we went back to the home church where they were hosting a nationally aired television broadcast on a major Christian network. As soon as I walked in the building, one of the pastors approached me and asked if I was the pastor he had heard about. I said "I guess so!" He then said I was going to share my testimony on national and international television that same night, and I did just that. Praise the Lord! The irony of all of this was that it was a very large church, and there were countless teams that went out that day. I never approached anyone, and I was not even wearing a suit. What made me so unique that they would call on me to testify? It was the favor of God. The favor of God on my life increased my visibility with people who were in a position to promote me. We were just starting out in ministry at this time and no one really knew who we were—but God knew who we were! This kind of visibility and preference is available to every believer on a consistent basis if we learn how to rightly discern the favor of God.

> *The favor of God on my life increased my visibility*
> *with people who were in a position to promote me.*

DISCERNING GOD'S FAVOR

As you read this book, the favor of God is going to be activated and released in your life. Remember, our father Abraham lived in a consistent flow of God's favor and we have been given access to this supernatural lifestyle in Christ. If we are in covenant relationship with God, then we ought to live in that same dimension of grace. The key in Abraham's life was his ability to discern the favor of God. In the same token, the key to us walking in God's supernatural favor is to discern that favor on our lives.

How do we discern God's favor? The Bible tells us in James 2:23, "And the scripture was fulfilled which saith, Abraham believed God, and it was imputed unto him for righteousness: and he was called the Friend of God." This is a very powerful statement! God referred to Abraham as His friend. Through Jesus Christ we have also been given the title of friend. Jesus said in the Gospel of John chapter 15 verse 15, "Henceforth I call you not servants; for the servant knoweth not what his lord doeth: but I have called you friends; for all things that I have heard of My Father I have made known unto you." We are no longer servants, we are actually the friends of God.

> *The key in Abraham's life was his ability*
> *to discern the favor of God.*

What does it mean to be a friend of God? This word comes from the Greek word *philos* (Strong's, G5384), which means to be friendly to, or to wish one well. It is a position of favor and intimacy. A friend has the proximity necessary to hear and perceive things that others cannot. A friend has privileges and rights that others do not. God has called us into this intimate relationship with Himself. This is a major promise, not to be taken lightly! It is this intimacy that was the impetus for Abraham discerning God's favor on his life. In fact, there was so much intimacy between Abraham and God, that Abraham negotiated the destruction of Sodom and Gomorrah (see Genesis 18:23-33). Can you imagine this? That Abraham had such an audience with the Creator of the universe. The implication is that God would have gone to the uttermost because of His relationship with Abraham.

The great news is that God is willing to do this for you as well. We have access to that same intimacy and it is through this intimacy that we discern the favor of God in our lives. When we use the term discern, we simply mean to perceive, recognize, or distinguish. Even though the favor of God is available to us, it takes recognition to activate it in our lives. Did you know that our Christian walk is supposed to be easy? It is not because we don't go through challenges, it is easy because we are walking in God's favor. This favor brings an end to striving in our own strength and ability. I don't know about you, but I want every drop of favor that God is willing to pour out. This Favor Factor gives us a strategic advantage over the world system. You and I can live a life filled with joy and peace because we have learned to be intimate with our heavenly Father, and have in turn recognized His favor at work in our lives.

FAVOR DECLARATION

Hallelujah! I declare in the name of Jesus Christ that I no longer trust in my own ability; from this day onward I activate God's favor in my life. Just as Joseph was set apart and blessed everywhere he went, I walk in a supernatural flow of favor everywhere I go. I thank You, Lord, for giving me favor with God and man. I declare that doors are open to me everywhere I go. I thank You, Lord, that I am Your friend and I have intimacy with You; therefore your goodness and favor goes before me and surround me. In Jesus' name. Amen!

Chapter 3

AN OPEN HEAVEN

The LORD shall open unto thee His good treasure,
the heaven to give the rain unto thy land in his
season, and to bless all the work of thine hand:
and thou shalt lend unto many nations, and
thou shalt not borrow (Deuteronomy 28:12).

S O FAR WE HAVE EXAMINED SEVERAL DYNAMICS OF SUPERNATURAL favor. If you are anything like me, you have wrestled with this idea during different times in your life. Why are there so many believers who struggle to get by day in and day out? Why are there so many people who seem to be wishing and hoping that God will bless them "If it is His will"? Is it really possible to live under an open heaven? I have asked all of these questions and more.

Like Abraham, I have had to follow God's instruction into seemingly impossible situations. Through every situation, God has shown Himself to be more faithful than I could have ever imagined. I believe that the favor of God is so much more than we have realized. We are living in a season where ignorance of this kind of favor could be detrimental to our well-being. I don't know about you, but I am determined to live under an open heaven for the rest of my life.

What do I mean by the expression open heaven? In Deuteronomy 28:12, God told the descendants of Abraham, the Israelites, that He would open His good treasure, the heaven, to give rain unto thy land in his season. What does this mean? For ancient Semitic people, heaven was one of the most important sources of life and well-being at that time. As a matter of fact, the word heavens is the Hebrew word *shamayim* (Strong's, H8064) and it is translated visible heavens or sky. This was so important because most people living in the ancient Middle East region were primarily agricultural farmers. Without rain, there were no crops, and without crops there was no food or livelihood. So we see that the promise of an open heaven was massive.

The Bible says that God will open His "good treasure." The word treasure in the Hebrew is *otsar* (Strong's, H214), which means treasury or storehouse. God promises that He will cause those who are in covenant relationship with Him to live under an open storehouse (heaven). This open heaven is a portal of favor, prosperity, increase, and blessing. When we live under an open heaven, we are living under a cloud of continued refreshment and provision. This was not meant to be a "one-time" blessing; it was meant to stay open, so long as the Israelites continued to obey God. The Bible goes further to say that God will bless all the work of our hands. Can you imagine living in a constant state of success? Can you imagine being in a position where all of the works of your hand are made to prosper? Well, this is exactly what the New Covenant believer has access to on a regular basis. This is supernatural favor!

Unlike the Israelites, this open heaven is not just a matter of us keeping God's commandment; it is a matter of covenant relationship. We have a covenant with God. This does not mean that we will automatically walk under an open heaven; but if we learn to recognize, acknowledge, and respond to the Word of God, we can live in the flow of heaven's storehouse. What is a storehouse? A storehouse is defined as a building for keeping goods of any kind, especially provisions; a magazine; a repository; a warehouse; a mass or quality laid up. This is a powerful truth! It is telling us that the heavens have everything that we need. This is not just a storehouse of physical blessings; it is a storehouse for whatever is needed, whenever it's needed. Or to say it another way, it is a mass laid up. The more we are conscious of the open heaven above us, the more we can place a demand on it. The more we place a demand on heaven's storehouse, the more we receive a supply of the blessing.

> *The more we are conscious of the open heaven above us, the more we can place a demand on it.*

RAIN IN *YOUR* LAND

There is an element to this promise that I neglected to pay attention to for a long time. For years, I struggled in my life, finances, and vocation; not realizing that there was so much more to the Christian life than difficulty. What was I missing? I did not pay attention to Deuteronomy 28:12 where it said, "to give the rain unto thy land in his season." What does it mean for God to give us the rain unto our land in its season? It was already mentioned that the rain represents a source of refreshment, harvest, and increase. If you have never experienced a drought, then it is difficult for you to appreciate the rain. In a place like ancient Palestine, rain is a precious commodity.

So God promises us rain; this is something that we all shout about, but there are two other elements to this promise that we often miss. The first one is that God says He will give the rain unto thy—*your*—*land*. What does this mean? This is the Hebrew word *erets* (Strong's, H776), and it not only means earth, but it also means country, region, or territory. God does not say that He will send the rain everywhere, but He has predetermined a specific location in which He will shower His favor and blessing. In other words, in order to experience this "rain," you and I must be in the exact spot that God has assigned.

What I did not realize for so many years is that the reason I was only receiving drops and not a deluge is because I was out of divine positioning. It is critical that you and I as born-again believers be in the right position. As a matter of fact, this is the technical definition of righteousness; right standing or right positioning. The reason why God is favorable toward us is not based on our performance for Him, but it is based on our position in Christ. In the same way, our ability to receive what heaven has to offer is based on us positioning ourselves correctly.

What is the right position to walk in God's supernatural favor? Obedience! When we are in the geographic location called obedience, we are postured to receive the fullness of what God wants us to experience. Did you know that God has already established a place of favor and blessing for every believer? It is what I call divine appointment. God has already commissioned the people, resources, and open doors that you need, but the key is to be exactly where God wants you.

For years I did not experience the fullness of God's blessings because I was out of position. I was running from my God-ordained assignment. God called me into the ministry at an early age, but because I did not want to be a preacher, I ran from this calling. I wanted to be a businessman, so I went to school to do just that. For a time I did well; I was experiencing the splashes of God's provision, but there was no deluge. After years of striving to be successful in business, I realized that it was not working for me. I was gifted and talented, but there was no supernatural grace on what I was doing. What was the problem? I was out of divine positioning. God already had my provision reserved in a predetermined spot, and in order to experience this I needed to walk in obedience to His Word.

Disobedience moves us out of our divine positioning. It is not that God closes the door, but the rain is falling in Utah and we are many times praying for the rain in California. This is why the dimension of intimacy is so important when it comes to supernatural favor, because intimacy enables us to be sensitive to what God is saying. The most blessed and favorable place that you and I could ever be is in the will of our heavenly Father. Obedience positions us to receive!

This is what it means to receive the rain in *your land*. It is a divine territory where you will experience more than enough.

When I finally caught on to this revelation, it changed my life. To illustrate this point I want to share with you something that happened to me several years ago. I was working in corporate America at the time, and my wife was a stay-at-home mother. It was financially challenging for us (I will talk about financial favor in more detail in a later chapter). God was really impressing the calling to ministry on our lives stronger than ever at this time. One night we came home from a speaking engagement that I had, and as we pulled into the driveway, my wife received a boldness from the Lord. She said to me, "I am tired of you running from the calling of God, it's time for you to be obedient. Stop making excuses!" Her words gripped my heart. I was both insulted and challenged in the same moment.

Later that night, I walked the streets of our subdivision; and as I walked, I began to surrender to the Lord. I asked God what He wanted from me, and I heard a still small voice that said, "I want *you!*" To this I responded by weeping and lying flat on the concrete. In that divine moment I surrendered to the call of God. I finally said yes! The next day, I was in my home on Saturday afternoon and felt led to go and check the mailbox. As I was looking through the mail I saw an envelope addressed to me from the company where I worked. When I opened the envelope there was a message from the company's CEO, "In celebration of our 50th anniversary and to celebrate you as an employee, we are depositing one thousand dollars directly into your bank account, tax free." Praise the Lord! I was amazed. This is exactly what we needed to meet an immediate expense that we had. Was this a coincidence? Why did this happen? I was receiving the rain in *my* land. The moment I surrendered to the call of God in obedience, I was postured to receive the abundant supply of His favor. Now that's supernatural favor!

> *The moment I surrendered to the call of God in obedience, I was postured to receive the abundant supply of His favor. Now that's supernatural favor!*

RAIN IN *YOUR* SEASON

The second aspect of this powerful revelation that I neglected for so many years, was not only that the rain was designated to a specific territory (in your land), but that the rain of God's favor and blessing would come in its season. The word season is the Hebrew word *eth* (Strong's, H6256, H5703) and it means time. What does it mean to receive the rain in our time (season)? The idea is that there is not only a divine place, but there is a divine time. Understanding the time of the rain is just as important as understanding the location of the rain. As a matter of fact, these two dimensions work in concert with each other. Any farmer will tell you that the timing is essential to reaping a harvest. My mentor said frequently, "Delayed obedience is disobedience!" Nothing could be more true.

When we have postured ourselves to obey the Word of God, the second step is to become sensitive to the timing of God. This is what the Bible is speaking of when it talks about rain in season. The Bible says in Psalm 1:3, "And he shall be like a tree planted by the rivers of water, that bringeth forth his fruit in his season; his leaf also shall not wither; and whatsoever he doeth shall prosper." The Bible tells us that the fruit promised to the blessed person will come in season. We see that there is a connection between our ability to receive from God and God's divine timing.

> *When we have postured ourselves to obey the Word of God, the second step is to become sensitive to the timing of God.*

There was a time my wife and I were being challenged in ministry and in finances. One day there was a meeting that I had scheduled, which was an hour and a half away from where I lived. We were low on funds at the time, about $100, but I had already scheduled the meeting so I was disposed to attend; besides, God told me to go specifically. Not only was I low on cash, but I also found out at the last minute that my tire needed to be fixed. Furthermore, our mortgage payment was over thirty days past due. This was quite a situation to say the least. We were believing God to come through in a significant way. I remember telling God, "YOU HAVE TO DO SOMETHING TODAY!" and "something" He did!

On the way to Orlando I had to change my tire, which cost me a substantial amount of money then I had to stop and get gas. This did not seem to be going as well as I anticipated. Finally, when I arrived at my meeting location, the person I was meeting was over an hour and a half late. Now I was definitely not in the best mood! After the minister arrived, we had a wonderful lunch meeting. There were words of encouragement and prophecy. It was amazing! When it was time to pay, I was praying that the minister would cover the cost of lunch, seeing I drove such a long way to meet with him; right? Wrong! The minister insisted on two separate checks. Now I was in an awkward situation.

Nonetheless, I swallowed my anxiety and decided that it was fine to pay for my own meal. Then came a mysterious turn of events. Right before I was about to pay the waiter, the Holy Spirit spoke to me and said, "I want you to pay for his meal as well." At first I debated internally with the Holy Spirit. I tried to convince the Lord that it was not such a great idea. Then I heard the Holy Spirit's voice again saying, "Pay for his meal!" Reluctantly I obeyed. Before I could give both of our checks to the server for payment, the minister reached over and prayed for me and said, "Lord, cause Kynan to walk under an open heaven! In Jesus' name. Amen!" Wow! I left that restaurant with an overwhelming sense of peace that I cannot describe to you. I was still upset about the situation, but I could not shake the peace of God inside me.

As I was driving home, I kept telling God that He had to do something about our financial situation. The next day, to my surprise, I received a call from someone asking me about the mortgage. Nothing had changed on my end, but the person said to me, "I am going to pay on this mortgage for you." The next day, I received another phone call from the same person, telling me that they were not only going to pay my past-due mortgage payment, but they were also going to pay my next payment as well. That was two mortgage payments. Hallelujah to the Lamb of God! How did that happen? It is very simple; I was sensitive to God's divine timing. When I thought it was time to reap, it was actually time to sow. I was expecting to receive, but it was God's divine timing to give. Attached to my response to God's timing was the rain that we were long awaiting.

This is what it means to receive rain in *your* season. There is a divine schedule associated with every blessing, and our ability to receive those blessings is contingent upon our sensitivity to this timing. What would have occurred if I was insensitive to the Holy Spirit? I would have missed the rain. God was setting me up to receive everything that He had for me, but it came in the form of giving a specific thing at a specific time. I was walking under an open heaven. God opened the heavens the moment the supplication was made, but I had to respond by discerning the timing of God.

You may be in this same position now. You are asking God why you have not received your breakthrough or your blessing yet. The key is obedience and sensitivity to the timing of God. If God told you that there was $1 million for you at a particular bank at a particular time (for example, between 7 AM – 8 AM) then receiving that $1 million would only be possible if you showed up at the right time. There is so much favor on your life right now! You just need to learn to recognize it and do what God tells you to do, when He tells you to do it—no matter what! In doing so, you will experience a deluge of favor and blessing that you have never experienced before. It's your season to walk under an open heaven!

FAVOR DECLARATION

Thank You, Lord, that You have promised to give me Your good treasure, the heaven. I declare in the name of Jesus that I walk under an open heaven. I declare that I have rain in my land in my season. I declare that my land is blessed and fruitful and the heaven over me is open. Therefore I declare that there are no limits to God's supernatural favor, His blessing, and divine increase in my life. In Jesus' name. Amen!

Chapter 4

ALL GRACE ABOUNDS

*And God is able to make **all grace abound**
toward you; that ye, always having all
sufficiency in all things, may abound to
every good work* (2 Corinthians 9:8).

Every Christian in the United States has probably read or heard of Second Corinthians 9:8, even if they were unaware of hearing it. The reason being is that this passage is usually associated with giving and often quoted. When I was growing up, I heard this passage every Sunday in church right before the offering plate was passed around. After a period of time I became desensitized to its application in my life. Could there be more to this passage of Scripture than meets the eye? What if I told you that understanding this Scripture verse could permanently transform your life?

There is a key in Second Corinthians 9:8 that unlocks the power of God's supernatural favor. I believe that there is a great revolution coming to the body of Christ. I like to call it a "Favor Revolution." This is going to be a radical and widespread experience of the supernatural favor of God in a way that we have never seen before. God wants us to experience His abounding grace on a daily basis. What do I mean when speaking of "abounding grace"? I explained earlier that favor and grace are many times interchangeable, but I want to take a few moments to break down the New Testament understanding of grace.

As mentioned previously, grace is often expressed as unmerited favor; however, grace is so much more. The Greek word for grace used in the New Testament is the word *charis* (Strong's, G5485). This word is defined as that which affords, favor, joy, charm, or delight. It is also translated benefit, bounty, or divine influence. In short, grace is the goodwill of God toward people, which manifests itself as supernatural power working in and on our behalf. This grace or favor produces joy and delight. This grace is multifaceted and multidimensional. For example, there is a dimension of grace that you and I experienced in becoming born again. In fact, Ephesians 2:8-9 says, "By grace are ye saved through faith; and that not of yourselves: it is the gift of God: not of works, lest any man should boast." This is what many scholars refer to as saving or delivering grace. This is the supernatural favor of God demonstrated in saving us.

When we come to Christ by faith, we experience this dimension of the favor of God. This grace was ushered in by Jesus Christ Himself. The Bible says that "the law was given by Moses, but grace and truth came by Jesus Christ" (John 1:17). Before we came to Christ, we were hell-bound sinners who were rescued from the grip of satan through the sovereign power of God. This is really the first aspect of God's favor that we experience as Christians.

Then there is a dimension of grace that enables us to stand in a position of righteousness. An example of this would be what Paul mentions in Romans 5:2, where he says, "By whom also we have access by faith into this grace wherein we stand, and rejoice in hope of the glory of God." This grace enables us to stand in a position pleasing to God, which includes the ability to overcome sin and failure in our lives. We call this "keeping grace."

Then there is another dimension of God's grace that meets our physical and financial needs. We see this demonstrated in Philippians 4:19 where it says, "My God shall supply all your need according to His riches in glory by Christ Jesus." This is what many refer to as provisional or special grace (we will talk about this dimension of grace in great detail in a later chapter).

As you can see, there are many dimensions to the unmerited favor of God. The question is, which dimension of grace can we experience in our lives at any given time? The answer is *all of them!* The Bible tells us in Second Corinthians 9:8 that God is able to make *all grace* abound toward us. What does it mean for all grace to abound toward a believer? In the original Greek the concept of all grace is expressed as "every favor and earthly blessing." I want you to take a few moments and think about the supernatural ramifications of every favor and earthly blessing abounding toward you. This is a tremendous promise of God. In fact, we need to take a closer look at this promise.

I love the fact that the Scripture precedes with the statement "and God is able." Do you realize that your God is able? It's as if Paul is reminding us that our God can do the miraculous. The word able there is expressed through a powerful Greek word *dynatos* Strong's, G1415. This word literally means to be powerful, mighty, strong, or to be mighty in wealth and influence. This is wonderful! When the Bible says that God is able, it means that God has all the power necessary to get the job done; not only that, but God also owns all of the resources. Am I saying that God can do anything? Absolutely! No matter what it is we are facing, God has the resources, ability, and influence to address that particular situation in our lives.

> *When the Bible says that God is able, it means that God has all the power necessary to get the job done; not only that, but God also owns all of the resources.*

The Bible goes further to say that this all-powerful God possesses the influence and ability to make *all grace* abound *toward* us. What does this mean? Can you imagine being in a position of having an all-powerful God enabling all the favor that He has at His disposal, in every form it exists, to work mightily in and on your behalf at all times? Well, I am here to tell you that this is not a fantasy or a figment of your imagination; this is reality for every New Covenant believer. This promise means that every dimension of favor that's available is already working on your behalf. Hallelujah!

I love the word "abound," because it implies an excess, overflow, and abundance of something. This grace not only comes to us in every form it is available, but it also comes to us in excess, overflow, and abundance. So whatever you need, whenever you need it, it is available to you in overflowing measure. The real power of this promise is the fact that God says that this *all grace* abounds toward us. When the Bible uses the word "toward," that means that the favor of God is pointed in our direction. Do you realize that God has literally commanded every blessing in heaven and earth to work in our favor? This means that we can never be victims of our circumstances ever again! There is nothing that the favor of God cannot accomplish for us.

Imagine for a moment you had a compass in your hand. No matter where you go that compass will always tell you where north is, because it is designed to point north at all times. This is what the Bible is conveying to us when it tells us that God's grace abounds toward us. The moment we came into covenant relationship with God, His goodness was permanently pointed in our direction. God's favor is toward us, not away from us.

I discovered that most Christians wrestle not with the question of whether or not God is able, but with the question, will He do it for me? The answer is an absolute yes! God will definitely do it for you! His power, love, provision, and blessing are always pointed in your direction. Open your heart and receive His favor right now.

EL SHADDAI (THE MANY BREASTED ONE)

There are many names of God throughout the Old Testament of the Bible that reveal a specific dimension of God's nature. Earlier, we talked about Abraham, and God's covenant promise that He made with him. We found out that this was a covenant of favor and blessing that God placed upon Abraham that has been transferred to us through the shed blood of Jesus Christ. In other words, we are children of Abraham. It is important for us then, to understand how God revealed Himself to the father of our faith.

In the book of Genesis chapter 15, verse 1, God revealed Himself to Abraham, "After these things the word of the LORD came unto Abram in a vision, saying, Fear not, Abram: I am thy shield, and thy exceeding great reward." God told Abram that He was his shield and "exceeding great reward." Wow! When you read this passage in the original Hebrew, you will see that this phrase great reward literally means to become much, or to become numerous. God told Abram (later Abraham) that He was going to become numerous to him. This not only implied that God would make him great in number, but that He would also reveal the multiplicity of His nature to Abraham. This was a promise that invited Abraham to experience the various dimensions of God's goodness that we spoke of earlier.

This alone would be enough for us to be thankful about, but God did not stop there. The Bible says in Exodus 6:2-3 that God was known to Abraham, Isaac, and Jacob by a specific name. Names are very significant in the Bible because they reveal the character of God. This specific name is also a source of power, because when you know the name of God, you are able to place a demand on that particular dimension of His nature. In fact, the Bible tells us exactly what that name is: "And God spake unto Moses, and said unto him, I am the LORD: and I appeared unto Abraham, unto Isaac, and unto Jacob, by the name of God Almighty, but by My name JEHOVAH was I not known to them" (Exodus 6:2-3). The Bible tells us that God was known unto Abraham by the name God Almighty. This is the Hebrew word *El Shaddai,* and it literally means "All Sufficient Source" or "The Many Breasted One" (*El*, Strong's, H410; *Shadday*, Strong's, H7706).

In other words, once we are in covenant relationship with God, He becomes the source of everything we need. God's goodness is demonstrated toward us in more ways than we can count. This is the essence of God's supernatural favor. Whatever we need, He is El Shaddai. God is not just favorable to us based on what we do, but He is favorable toward us because He is good-natured. Furthermore, when we come into a covenant relationship with God, He obligates Himself to displaying that goodness toward us. Just as a father is obligated to provide everything that his children need, God our Father is obligated to pour out His favor on us in every area of our lives so long as we surrender to Him.

> *In other words, once we are in covenant relationship with God, He becomes the source of everything we need. God's goodness is demonstrated toward us in more ways than we can count.*

When my oldest daughter was born, my my wife chose to breast-feed her. My daughter grew very fast and very rarely had any colds or other problems. We discovered that breast milk has just about everything a child needs to grow up and be strong. Isn't it amazing that a simple yet consistent diet of breast milk could make a baby grow so much? Why is this the case? It's very simple! The milk is packed with vitamins, minerals, and nutrients. My wife's breasts were a source of sufficiency for our daughter.

In the same manner, God is our source of strength, nourishment, and increase. The key is learning how to draw from that source. What most lactation specialists will tell you is that the production of breast milk is based on a concept called supply and demand. So, the more the child drinks the mother's breast milk, the more breast milk she produces. If the child only drinks a small amount, only a small amount will be supplied. It is the same in our relating to God as El Shaddai; the more we place a demand on this dimension of His grace, the more we will see it demonstrated in our lives. Whatever you need Him to be, He can be it if you will approach Him with expectation.

For years, I sat back and suffered because I did not know what it meant for all grace to abound to me. God is just waiting on us to approach Him with expectation. If only the body of Christ would grasp this revelation, we would no longer have to walk around in defeatism and despondency—we would know that we have access to a supernatural, all-sufficient source of favor, provision, protection, and blessing. He is more than enough! Our father Abraham walked in this reality all the days of his life. Not only did Abraham walk in this dimension of God's goodness, but also his children and grandchildren, Isaac and Jacob. So when the Bible tells us that the blessing of Abraham has come on the Gentiles by faith, it is actually telling us that we have been given permission to know God as El Shaddai. He is our all-sufficient source! This is not some far out promise that we are unable to grasp—this is reality. To further illustrate this point, I will share a testimony with you.

A TESTIMONY OF FAVOR

Before I was born, my mother was diagnosed with multiple sclerosis (MS). As I progressed into my teen years, my mother's condition became very severe. In fact, I remember one particular night my mother had an MS attack. This attack caused a blood clot in my mother's lungs. She went in and out of consciousness for hours. She could not remember any of her children's names except myself and my brother. I was very distraught to say the least.

I was just becoming acclimated with the understanding of divine healing at this time, but at least I knew enough to pray and declare the blood of Jesus. Later that night they rushed my mother to the intensive care unit of a major hospital in Atlanta, Georgia. I remember waiting in the lobby praying for my mother while hearing the news that she may not survive. *Oh Lord, what are we going to do?* The blood clot was traveling through her body and had the potential to end her life. I went into the room with my mother and watched her drift in and out of consciousness. I prayed and asked God for a miracle; I asked for His favor to abound toward my mother.

Then an amazing thing happened.

As I was sitting in the room with my mother, the pastor of our church came into the room. As soon as he entered, my mother awoke from unconsciousness and said, "El Shaddai!" To this the pastor replied, "That's right, El Shaddai." Immediately, my mother was supernaturally healed. Several hours later, my mother was released from the hospital with no blood clot in her lungs. Hallelujah!

> *God's favor has the power to touch every area of our lives. He is truly God Almighty!*

That day, I learned a very powerful lesson; God's favor has the power to touch every area of our lives. He is truly God Almighty! The challenge that we often have is believing that He is exactly who He says. If we will simply place a demand on this favor, we will be surprised at how effectually it will work in and through our lives. God is truly able to make all grace abound!

FAVOR DECLARATION

Father, in the name of Jesus I thank You that Your word says that You will cause all grace to abound toward me. I thank You that it is Your will and desire to bless me. I receive Your abundance of grace today, and therefore receive the supernatural power of God at work in me. And because of Your grace, I stand in a favorable position in Your eyes. Lord, You are my all-sufficient source, my El Shaddai who liberally and abundantly supplies "all" my needs. In the name of Jesus, Amen.

Chapter 5

FAVOR AS OUR BIRTHRIGHT

Blessed be the God and Father of our Lord Jesus Christ, who hath blessed us with all spiritual blessings in heavenly places in Christ (Ephesians 1:3).

IF YOU ARE NOT EXCITED ABOUT THE FAVOR OF GOD BY NOW, YOU might not be alive; we may need to have a resurrection prayer at the end of this book! I am thoroughly convinced that your life will never be the same once you receive an impartation of the supernatural favor of God that we have talked about thus far.

In my book, *Possessing Your Healing: Taking Authority Over Sickness in Your Life,* I talk about the pressure that many people feel when it comes to divine healing. They believe that the burden of healing lies on their shoulders; therefore, they find it difficult to believe God for their healing or the healing of their loved ones. The truth is that our healing is not a religious act that we perform—it is an inheritance that we receive. In the same way, our ability to receive and walk in God's favor is not based on merit—it is our birthright.

When we throw around terms like birthright, what are we actually talking about? Webster's Dictionary defines a birthright as a particular right of possession or privilege one has from birth. What is a right of possession or privilege? Let's look at this for a moment. A right is something that we have a legal entitlement to. As Americans, we are quite familiar with the U.S. Constitution. The Constitution outlines our rights as citizens of this nation. When you know that something is a right, you can place a demand on it. The second aspect is that of privilege. A privilege carries with it the connotation of a special right, benefit, or advantage. So we have been given specific rights, benefits, and advantages.

When were these rights and privileges given to us? They were given to us from birth; the new birth that is! The moment we became born again, we received a divine inheritance from God that gave us the legal right to place a demand on particular privileges and blessings. In the book of Ephesians, we see this biblical truth masterfully expressed by Apostle Paul, under the divine inspiration of the Holy Spirit. In the first chapter of Ephesians, the third verse says, "Blessed be the God and Father of our Lord Jesus Christ, who hath blessed us with all spiritual blessings in heavenly places in Christ." Many have read this Scripture before, but many probably don't have a strong grasp of its true meaning.

> *The moment we became born again, we received a divine inheritance from God that gave us the legal right to place a demand on particular privileges and blessings.*

What does it mean to be blessed with all spiritual blessings in heavenly places in Christ? To better understand this verse, it may help to examine it from a Jewish perspective. Paul, being a devout Jew and Pharisee, is alluding to the concept of the birthright found in Hebrew culture. In Jewish culture, the inheritance of a father's estate was primarily vested in the eldest son. This is called a birthright. We see this illustrated in the life of Jacob, in Genesis 25:31-33, when Jacob purchased the birthright from his older brother Esau. In fact, the birthright was much more than just a physical inheritance. The Bible tells us in Genesis 27 that Rebekah put the raiment of Esau on Jacob and placed the skin of a hairy animal on his skin; what took place after this was amazing. This is what the Bible says:

> *And Jacob went near unto Isaac his father; and he felt him, and said, The voice is Jacob's voice, but the hands are the hands of Esau. And he discerned him not, because his hands were hairy, as his brother Esau's hands: so he blessed him. And he said, Art thou my very son Esau? And he said, I am. And he said, Bring it near to me,*

and I will eat of my son's venison, that my soul may bless thee. And he brought it near to him, and he did eat: and he brought him wine, and he drank. And his father Isaac said unto him, Come near now, and kiss me, my son. And he came near, and kissed him: and he smelled the smell of his raiment, and blessed him, and said, See, the smell of my son is as the smell of a field which the LORD hath blessed: Therefore God give thee of the dew of heaven, and the fatness of the earth, and plenty of corn and wine: Let people serve thee, and nations bow down to thee: be lord over thy brethren, and let thy mother's sons bow down to thee: cursed [be] every one that curseth thee, and blessed be he that blesseth thee (Genesis 27:22-29).

This birthright was a spiritual blessing. Isaac decreed over Jacob's life that God would give him of the dew of heaven (favor, blessing, and provision) and the fatness of the earth, and plenty of corn and wine (divine prosperity). Isaac also declared that nations would bow down and serve him and that he would be lord over his brothers. Wow! What a blessing! The father literally spoke well over his son, and that oral blessing set spiritual forces in motion that would work favorably on the son's behalf.

This is exactly what the Bible is talking about in Ephesians 1:3. In fact, the word blessing is the Greek word *eulogia* (Strong's, G2129) which means to speak well of someone. When people are eulogized at a funeral, the preacher says only good things about them. In the same manner, God has spoken well of us. In fact, we are able to partake of this spiritual blessing because of Jesus Christ. Ephesians tells us that this *eulogia* or blessing has been given to us in Christ. Esau was the eldest son entitled to the birthright, but he transferred his birthright to the youngest son; this was a type and shadow.

Jesus Christ is the eldest son in redemption and He has received the birthright from God the Father and has transferred that birthright to us. Matthew 3:17 says, "And lo a voice from heaven, saying, This is my beloved Son, in whom I am well pleased." God is well pleased with His firstborn Son Jesus Christ. Jesus is the beloved of God. Through the blood of Jesus Christ, you and I are the beloved of God and the same favor and blessing on Jesus Himself has been transferred to us. This favor is not just available to us sometimes; it is a right and a privilege!

BELOVED IN OUR FATHER'S EYES

I am the youngest of five siblings, and as such I received much preferential treatment from my parents. This is an almost inescapable reality of birth order. I remember when it was time for me to graduate from high school. My mother had an Acura Legend V6 sedan. It was gold with alloy rims and a full leather interior; I can still smell the leather right now! All of my siblings were vying for ownership of that car. My mother turned them all down. She said that she was keeping that car for herself. Then, I am sure you can imagine the vehement anger and frustration that they expressed toward my mother once they found out that she was giving it to me. There was nothing that I did to deserve that car, I was simply in the right position; a position of favor in my mother's eyes. She favored me as her last-born son, not to mention the fact that I was a very unique child (to say the least). I had a special place in my mother's heart and this was evident to all.

In the same way, you and I have found favor in the eyes of our heavenly Father, and it should be evident to all. This favor is not about what we have done to deserve it, it is based on our position; a position of righteousness. This doesn't mean that we can live any kind of way that we like and still expect to have God's best for our lives, but it does mean that God is relating to us based on a favorable attitude that He has toward us because of Jesus Christ. In the order of redemption, we would be considered His last-born children. Like most last borns, God has reserved the best for last. We are blessed of our Father! It is just that simple.

> *We have been so accustomed to formulas and mechanics that we have neglected the simple truth that the moment you and I became born again, we were supernaturally thrust into a position of favor and blessing.*

Unfortunately, many simple things are very difficult to receive due to their simplicity. We have been so accustomed to formulas and mechanics that we have neglected the simple truth that the moment you and I became born again, we were supernaturally thrust into a position of favor and blessing. This is why when most of us initially became born again, there was such a zeal and enthusiasm that we experienced. I for one can remember the flow of joy, blessings, and prosperity that I seemed to abide in effortlessly when I first came to Christ. Why was this the case? It is very simple! As newborn babes in Christ, we simply accepted the fact that God was exactly who He said He was, and He was on our side. Well, you and I can live in that flow every day of our lives. It is available to us right now! The key is knowing that God is pleased with you already! Just like my mother already decided that she was going to spoil me before I was even born, God has reserved favor, preferential treatment, and blessing in Christ before we ever became conscious of this truth.

FAVOR MULTIPLIED THROUGH KNOWLEDGE

Grace and peace be multiplied unto you through the knowledge of God, and of Jesus our Lord, According as His divine power hath given unto us all things that pertain unto life and godliness, through the knowledge of Him that hath called us to glory and virtue (2 Peter 1:2-3).

I am sure that you have probably heard the old adage, "What you don't know, won't hurt you." Actually, nothing could be further from the truth. In the kingdom of God, what you do not know can absolutely hurt you. Conversely, what you do know has the power to supernaturally bless your life. This is what Apostle Peter is talking about in the book of Second Peter. The Bible says that grace or favor is multiplied through the knowledge of God. What exactly does this mean? The word knowledge in that passage is the Greek word *epignosis* (Strong's, G1922) and it literally means precise or correct knowledge. This is not talking about general knowledge, but it is referring to specific knowledge based on revelation and insight. Another way of putting it would be to obtain understanding.

What is understanding? Understanding is defined as the ability to comprehend something. When you and I were in school, we had to take exams. The purpose of every exam was to measure our level of understanding or comprehension. It is not enough to just sit in a classroom and hear the principles that the instructors are presenting; we must have a precise level of comprehension. The same stands true when it comes to God. It is not enough for us to read the Bible every now and then or simply pay attention in Sunday school—our knowledge of God must be based on spiritual revelation and comprehension.

> *It is not enough for us to read the Bible every now and then or simply pay attention in Sunday school—our knowledge of God must be based on spiritual revelation and comprehension.*

The Bible says in Second Peter that when we possess this understanding, the favor of God will be multiplied in our lives. Which is to say, the more we know about our heavenly Father, the more His favor will be manifested in our lives. You may be wondering, *Pastor Kynan, are you saying that it is possible for God's grace to multiply?* According to the Word of God, yes! The word multiply simply means to increase. Did you know that people experience varying degrees of God's favor as a result of their level of knowledge? This is why there are some Christians who seem to get blessed all the time, while others seem to be in a constant struggle. Is God a respecter of persons? Does He play favorites? Absolutely not! Every born-again believer has access to the supernatural favor of God as their birthright, but they will only experience this favor when they know who their Father is and become conscious of what He has made available to them.

It is like many other forms of ignorance. The less people know about something, the less they can leverage that thing to work in their favor. For instance, many people are ignorant of how the human heart works. They have no clue what the aortic valve is, or the proper pressure levels that the heart needs to work efficiently. As a result, they are ignorant of how their diets affect their heart's health. Just as a poor diet can clog the valves of our hearts and in turn block the flow of oxygen in our bodies, incorrect knowledge of God can block His favor from flowing in our lives.

We must know exactly who our Father is and what He has for us. It literally breaks my heart to see so many believers living beneath the plan and purpose that God has for their lives. I don't know about you, but I want all that God has for me. What is the solution to this situation? We have to get to know our Father; and the best way to get to know our Father is to meditate in His Word. The more we discover His identity in the Word of God, the more we will experience this supernatural favor that He is so eager to pour out on us. God is waiting on you to take hold of this reality in your life today!

INVOKING OUR RIGHTS

When it comes to the supernatural favor of God, you and I have to learn how to invoke our rights. Some would ask, "Are you suggesting that we put a demand on God?" Absolutely! In fact, if you don't place a demand on your rights, oftentimes they will not be enforced. The Bible says that we are already blessed and favored by our heavenly Father; the key now is to start walking like it.

This concept may be completely countercultural to you. Religion and tradition have encouraged a certain level of passivity and laziness in churchgoers. We are taught to sit back and wait for God to do something while wishing and hoping that it happens soon. This is not the right attitude that we should possess. We must invoke our rights!

Years ago, when I was in the insurance business, I had to become very familiar with contract law. One very important facet of contract law was the concept of estoppel. This is a legal term which essentially implies the precluding or barring of a person from denying or asserting anything to the contrary of that which has been legally established as the truth. For example, in an insurance contract there is a premium paid to the insurer and a policy issued to the insured. When a person pays an insurance company money, the insurance company enters into a contractual agreement that they will provide certain benefits and payments consistent with the policy. If for any reason, other than that which is permitted in the policy, the insurance company seeks to deny a reasonable claim, the insurance company can be estopped from denying the claim by law based on the strength of the policy itself. In other words, the insured person has the ability to invoke his or her rights set forth in the contract.

> *Whenever the devil tries to take from us what is rightfully ours or deny us the life that Jesus paid a premium for, he must be stopped.*

It is the same for born-again believers. We entered into a covenant or contract with God based on the blood of Jesus Christ. Whenever the devil tries to take from us what is rightfully ours or deny us the life that Jesus paid a premium for, he must be stopped. You must understand that God wants you blessed, whole, and prosperous. It is satan that wants to rob you of what God has already given you. Stop him in his tracks! Favor is your birthright. You can live above situations and circumstances. You can live in a constant state of advantage and preferential treatment. Don't you dare settle for anything less!

FAVOR DECLARATION

Thank You, Lord, for the gift of sonship and blessing me with all spiritual blessings in heavenly places with Jesus. Thank You, Lord, for my supernatural inheritance of favor through the shed blood of Jesus. I declare that favor is multiplied toward me through the knowledge of Your Son Jesus Christ. I invoke my rights to walk in Your favor, and I receive, right now, a supernatural impartation of Your favor, in Jesus' name! Amen!

Chapter 6

FAITH AND FAVOR

Now faith is the substance of things hoped for,
the evidence of things not seen (Hebrews 11:1).

As you have probably realized by now, there is a direct
correlation between faith and supernatural favor. What is the
relationship between faith and favor? Faith is the means through
which we place a demand on and experience the favor of God.

Earlier we talked about the principle of supply and demand, and it
is important to understand how to tap into this spiritual reality. Our

faith in the Word of God is essential for us to walk in the promises of God for our lives. The writer of Hebrews says that faith is the substance of things hoped for and the evidence of things not seen. This Scripture verse is packed with supernatural power that can transform your life. The word faith is the Greek word *pistis* (Strong's, G4102), which means confidence or conviction. Simply put, you and I must be confident about the truth of God's Word.

The reason why we are able to walk in the supernatural favor of God is because it is a spiritual reality. When we use the term spiritual reality, we are simply referring to something that is a fixed reality from God's perspective. Remember, Jesus Christ is the impetus for divine favor in our lives. This confidence or conviction is the support for everything we believe and act upon. For example, when you and I wake up in the morning, we place our feet on the floor with the absolute confidence that we are not going to fall through the floor to our destruction. Why? It is because we are absolutely convinced that the foundation of the house can support our weight.

Faith is the same way! It is the absolute conviction that what God says about you and to you is the truth. This confidence is the support system that enables you to receive and stand upon the promises of God; it can support the weight of whatever you need!

When we have an attitude of faith, it creates expectation in our hearts. We begin to anticipate our expectation with great joy and delight. Many times when I wake up in the morning, I get excited about what God is going to manifest in my life that day, because I know that God is eager to display His goodness toward me. This attitude stands as the evidence of what I cannot physically see. The favor of God is invisible to the natural eyes, but we can see its effects. Like electricity, we cannot see it, but we know it is present. When it comes to God's supernatural favor, you and I have to be convinced that it is operating, regardless of physical circumstances.

Why do so many Christians see favor and blessing as something foreign to them? The reason why so many Christians do not experience the favor of God in their lives is because of unbelief. In my time of being in ministry, it seems like the word unbelief has become an offensive word. No one wants to be accused of being in unbelief! Religion has taught us that our faith is a deeply personal matter. Though faith is personal, its presence and effects are evident to all. We are either walking in faith or we are not. We either believe God's Word or we do not. It is really that simple! The moment we embrace the simplicity of faith is the moment we can walk in it with authenticity.

Many Christians don't believe that their lives should be any better than they are right now. Some people don't believe that God has already poured out favor and blessing on them because they are being controlled by their physical circumstances. The truth is that God's favor toward us is a spiritual reality; it's a biblical truth! It does not matter how things look on the outside. We received access to God's covenant of supernatural favor on Abraham through Jesus Christ. We inherited this favor! It belongs to us. We appropriate this favor by faith. In fact, the Bible says in Ephesians 2:8-9, "For by grace are ye saved through faith; and that not of yourselves: it is the gift of God: not of works, lest any man should boast." This is very powerful! The Word of God says that the favor of God, which delivers us and meets every need, is available to us through faith. The word through is the Greek word *dia* (Strong's, G1223) and it means the ground or reason by which something is or is not done. So we can say faith is the means or grounds by which we receive God's favor.

> *The truth is that God's favor toward us is a spiritual reality; it's a biblical truth! It does not matter how things look on the outside.*

Conversely, doubt and unbelief are grounds for not being able to walk in the favor of God. The Bible tells us in John 3:16 that, "God so loved the world that He gave His only begotten Son, that whosoever believeth in Him should not perish, but have everlasting life." This demonstrates to us that God loves everyone and sent Jesus Christ to die for the sins of the whole world—but only those who believe in Him will experience everlasting life. It is the same for us as believers. God has poured out an abundant supply of His favor and goodness on us through Jesus, but only those who receive it by faith will walk in this reality. The Bible tells us that this favor is the gift of God. It is not based on how well we perform—it is based on whether or not we believe. Abraham was counted righteous and entered into friendship with God by faith, before He was ever circumcised. This is why faith is essential to our ability to live in the supernatural favor of God on a regular basis.

FAVOR RELEASED THROUGH OUR WORDS

Did you know that the words we speak are vitally important? Did you know that our words have the power to create or bring destruction? The Bible says that "Death and life are in the power of the tongue: and they that love it shall eat the fruit thereof" (Proverbs 18:21). The word tongue is literally interpreted as hand in Hebrew. Let's look at this for a moment. Death and life are in the hand of the tongue? What does this mean? It means that our words are the architect of our environment.

Like a carpenter takes a hammer and nail and builds a home with his hands, our tongue builds the spiritual and physical environment around us. We will ultimately eat the fruit of our words! Another way of putting it is that we will live in the house we have built with our words. We previously discussed the fact that the birthright found in both Genesis and Ephesians is an oral blessing that sets spiritual forces in motion. When Isaac spoke over his son Jacob, his words set spiritual forces in motion that created an atmosphere of blessing and increase.

> *Favor has the power to cause someone to bless you or do something that benefits you in the natural realm; it also has the ability to cause us to experience God's supernatural power in our lives.*

Favor is a spiritual force that produces a tangible outcome. Favor has the power to cause someone to bless you or do something that benefits you in the natural realm; it also has the ability to cause us to experience God's supernatural power in our lives. This spiritual force of favor is released through the words that we speak. It is amazing to me how so many people neglect this simple biblical truth. Jesus said that it is not what goes into a person that defiles, but what comes out. Then it says in Luke 6:45, *"A good man out of the good treasure of his heart, bringeth forth that which is good; and an evil man out of the evil treasure of his heart, bringeth forth that which is evil: for of the abundance of the heart his mouth speaketh.*" The Bible is literally telling us that the internal repository of our hearts are manifested through what we speak. When we speak good, it is indicative of a right heart; when we speak evil, it is indicative of a wrong heart.

> *We will set promotion, preferential treatment, blessing, and supernatural ability in motion through what we speak forth.*

As a matter of fact, the word speak used in Luke 6:45 is the Greek word *prophero* (Strong's, G4393), which means to bring forth. We have been given the spiritual ability to "bring forth" that which is good through the words that we speak. Your words have the power to create a spiritual atmosphere of life or death around you. Imagine, if you will, a thermostat. What is the purpose of a thermostat? A thermostat regulates the temperature of a room or building. Once you set a specific temperature on the thermostat, it gradually creates an environment based on the temperature that was programmed into it. Our words are the same way. What we speak consistently determines the temperature, which in turn becomes our environment.

What does all of this have to do with supernatural favor? Job 22:28 tells us that we shall decree a thing and it shall be established. The more we begin to release faith-filled words into the atmosphere, the more we will create an environment of supernatural favor around us. We will set promotion, preferential treatment, blessing, and supernatural ability in motion through what we speak forth. You may say, "I just don't believe that!" Well of course you don't! You can never believe something that you are speaking against on a consistent basis. There is a direct correlation between our faith and our confession. I have seen this demonstrated a million times. People will say that this confession stuff doesn't work, yet they find themselves in the same negative, ill-favored state they have always been in. What is the problem? They are speaking death.

I remember being in a place where I would ask God for certain things to happen and when nothing would happen, I became frustrated. One day I was praying while frustrated, and the Spirit of God spoke to me and said, "I have been sending My angels of provision to come and minister to your need, but they come back and report that you have consistently changed addresses." I asked the Lord what He meant by this and He told me, "My angels hearken to the voice of the Word and every time they are about to show up and manifest what you were asking for, all they hear is murmuring and complaining. They assume that they have the wrong location because your words no longer line up with your original request."

When I heard this I was humiliated. I immediately asked God to forgive me for my negativity, doubt, and unbelief. God began to unfold to me that our words are the air traffic control of heaven. Just like planes in the natural must be guided into landing through a control tower, angelic assistance, promotion, increase, and divine help follow the directives of the words that we speak. I was the one responsible for the delayed answers to prayer and did not even realize it. One day I would thank God for His blessing and favor, and the next day I was complaining about my circumstances. Heaven responds to faith and to the Word of God. If we are to experience an open heaven over our lives, we have to learn to say what God says, and *only* what God says.

A WORD FITLY SPOKEN

A word fitly spoken is like apples of gold in pictures of silver (Proverbs 25:11).

We have seen that there are profound implications to the words that we speak, as well as the fact that faith is absolutely necessary in releasing the supernatural favor of God. Now I want us to examine our words a little further. When I was growing up, I was very small. I was the little kid in the classroom. As you may have guessed, people found it very humorous to pick on me. It wasn't until my middle school years that I realized I needed to come up with an offensive technique that would help me survive the rest of my school years. I discovered a mechanism that I like to call the "keep talking" mechanism. Whenever kids would pick on me, I could not rely on my physical stature, so I would just keep throwing a barrage of words at them until I won the verbal battle. It was really a matter of timing when you think about it.

I have since been delivered from the need to compensate with my words, but I learned a powerful spiritual principle; the right word spoken at the right time was very powerful. I discovered this Scripture in the Bible early on in my walk with Christ. Proverbs 25:11 says, "A word fitly spoken is like apples of gold in pictures of silver." This seems to be a very complex concept but it is not. When the Bible talks about a word "fitly" spoken, it is talking about more than just something that we arbitrarily say. The word fitly is a Hebrew compound word which combines two elements. The first is that of a wheel; that's right, wheel. It is the same word for wheel used in the book of Ezekiel to describe the prophet's vision. The word imagery here is that of a spinning wheel. In other words, our words (spoken in faith) create spiritual momentum. Previously, we talked about setting spiritual forces in motion; the key word is motion. Our words cause things to move in the spiritual realm.

The second component to this Hebrew word is that of timing. It is a word spoken at the right time. If you don't mind, I would like to give a sports analogy. When I was younger I played baseball. I can vividly remember going up to the plate when it was my turn at bat. What was the secret to hitting the ball out of the park? It was a matter of timing and momentum. In order to make a connection between the baseball and the bat, there had to be a combination of the right momentum and the right timing. In the same way, the Bible tells us that a word spoken with spiritual momentum and divine timing is like apples of gold in pictures of silver. Apples of gold in pictures of silver would be ornamental showpieces very beautiful to look at and probably only present in a royal or wealthy household. It represents favor.

Learning to say the right things, according to the Word, at the right time is a key to experiencing an even greater measure of God's supernatural favor in your life. To illustrate this point even further, I will share a story about a young man in our church. This young man had been with us for some time and received much insight from our teaching. God told our church to go on a 21-day fast. During this time, the Lord instructed me to only confess positively. So for 21 days the entire church engaged in positive biblical confession. It was during this time that there was a new manager brought into this young man's place of employment. As the new manager was reviewing the performance of the employees, his file came up. To his surprise, he was given a negative review. He had never had an adverse review before.

> *Learning to say the right things, according to the Word, at the right time is a key to experiencing an even greater measure of God's supernatural favor in your life.*

Due to the confession of God's Word that we were engaged in as a church, he was determined that he would not complain or murmur. Instead, he only spoke forth faith-filled words. He would tell himself every day that he had wonderful managers and an even more wonderful work environment. One day the manager asked him if she could take his department out to lunch; this was the same manager who had given him a negative evaluation. Coincidentally, she requested to ride in his car. During the drive to the restaurant, she asked him if he had any complaints about the other managers, to which he responded, "I do not engage in any form of gossip. I just focus on my assignments, because I am thankful to have this job." To this she replied, "Wow! That is very refreshing to hear!" A few days later she recommended him for a promotion. Several days later he received a promotion and a pay raise. Hallelujah!

The same manager who seemed to be a threat to his employment, was the same manager God used to give him divine promotion. What was the key? His words were fitly spoken! Instead of complaining and speaking negatively, he was sensitive to the Holy Spirit who enabled him to say the right thing at the right time. His words became the supernatural wheels God used to transport him to a place of favor and promotion. In his very mouth were "apples of gold." There is supernatural power in a word fitly spoken.

FAVOR DECLARATION

Father, in the name of Jesus, I thank You for who You are and all that You have done. Right now in the name of Jesus I decree and declare that I have great faith. In accordance with Mark 11:22-23, I have the God kind of faith, and every mountain in my life and in the lives of those around me must obey my voice. I open my mouth right now and I say that your favor and goodness overflows every area of my life; doubt and unbelief must go from me. I am a believer of the Word of God. Every Word in the Bible is the truth and I believe it. Your Word says that I am blessed and highly favored of the Lord, and I receive this promise. The Word of God is the final authority in my life. I am not moved by what I see—I am moved by the Word of God only. I walk by faith in the Word of God and not by sight. This divine faith releases Your supernatural favor in my life today. I am not controlled by my emotions, the emotions of others, or my environment—I am completely dominated by God's Word. Romans 10:17 declares that faith comes by hearing and hearing by the Word of God. I am a hearer of Your Word; and as a result, I have faith. Faith is the revelation of God's Word in action; therefore, I am a doer of Your Word. Nothing is impossible to me because I am a believer of Your Word.

Chapter 7

FINANCIAL FAVOR

And He commanded the multitude to sit down on the grass, and took the five loaves, and the two fishes, and looking up to heaven, He blessed, and brake, and gave the loaves to His disciples, and the disciples to the multitude (Matthew 14:19).

I LOVE READING THE GOSPELS—MATTHEW, MARK, LUKE, AND John. In them is a panoramic view of our Lord, His teachings, and His testimony. I believe that the Gospels give us an even more profound understanding of God's *Supernatural Favor.* Our Lord walked in this favor every day of His earthly ministry.

Have you ever asked yourself how someone who quit their full-time job as a carpenter to go into full-time ministry with just twelve members could survive for three and a half years? Some would say, "Oh, He was God!" We all agree that Jesus Christ was God in the flesh, this is essential to Christian theology, but this was not the only reason He was able to perform miracles and live supernaturally. The truth is that Jesus walked in the revelation of the Word of God, and was firmly convinced that the Father was exactly who He said He was. The favor of God on His life was a source of supernatural financial provision.

This is illustrated profoundly in the book of Matthew when Jesus, after ministering to a multitude, was asked by His disciples to send the multitude away. Why? Because the disciples did not have enough food to feed the people. Have you ever been in a situation like that? Have you ever looked at what you had, just to realize that it was not enough? This is exactly the position the disciples were in. They did not see a logical outcome in the natural realm. To this question, Jesus responded with a profound statement, "But Jesus said unto them, They need not depart; give ye them to eat" (Matthew 14:16). Why would Jesus say something like that? It was evident that they didn't have enough food, right? Wrong!

Remember, when we are walking in supernatural favor we always have *more than enough!* What was the secret Jesus knew that the disciples did not? He recognized the supernatural favor of God on His life and in that particular situation. Previously we talked about how faith activates the favor of God on our lives, and we know from the testimony of Scripture that Jesus was a Man of faith. What seemed like an impossible circumstance to the disciples was simply God's opportunity to demonstrate His goodness. Like most of us would do if we found ourselves in a situation of this magnitude, the disciples began to try and quantify what they had at their disposal. The best they could come up with was two fish and five loaves of bread (this was the equivalent of a lunch for a young boy). There were over 5,000 men, not even counting the women and children. What were the disciples to do? Jesus says in Matthew 14:18, "Bring them hither to me."

> *Remember, when we are walking in supernatural favor we always have more than enough!*

One of the first things we need to be convicted about as believers is that God is a supernatural God. What do I mean by this? This means that God has to place His *super* on our *natural!* Many Christians are struggling and frustrated with their financial lives because they refuse to allow God to magnetize what they have with His supernatural power. The favor of God has the power to magnetize what we have and cause it to be a source of attracting even greater provision. The first command that Jesus gave was to bring what we have to Him. This is more significant than you and I may realize.

For years, I suffered financially because I refused to bring what I had to God. Let me be clear, I am not simply talking about tithes and offerings (I have been a tither for years), I am talking about bringing everything. We must realize that everything in our possession belongs to God, and He has the right to do with it as He pleases. Interestingly enough, the Greek word for bring is the word *phero* (Strong's, G5342) and it means to carry or rush (as in something heavy or burdensome). This tells me that one of our biggest difficulties is not an issue of trusting that God can do the supernatural, but it is the challenge of bringing our natural to Him. When we don't bring what we have to the Lord, it becomes a burden. This is how we participate in the supernatural favor of God; we must submit what we have to Him. It doesn't matter how small it is! The word *phero* implies speed, which suggests that the faster we bring what we have to Him, the sooner we will experience His supernatural provision.

The next thing that Jesus did once the disciples brought what they had to Him was command everyone to sit down. Why did Jesus make everyone sit down? I believe it was twofold. The first reason was that He was fulfilling Psalm 23, "He maketh me to lie down in green pastures." Jesus was demonstrating to the disciples that He was and is the *Good Shepherd*. The second reason is that He wanted to teach us to lean on God's favor. The word for sit down is the Greek word *anaklino* (Strong's, G347), which means to lean against or recline. If we are going to experience financial favor, we have to learn to recline in God's grace, ability, and power, and stop trying to do things in our own might. This was a posture of humility and submission. It has nothing to do with natural quantities or limitations, it has everything to do with the substance of God's power.

> *If we are going to experience financial favor, we have to learn to recline in God's grace, ability, and power, and stop trying to do things in our own might.*

The next thing that Jesus did was bless the bread and fish. This is amazing! The Greek word for blessed of course is the word *eulogeo* (Strong's, G2127) which is the verb form of the same word found in Ephesians 1 and it means to praise, to cause to prosper, or to be favored of God. In this one statement is a biblical truth that literally transformed my life! The moment Jesus applied the favor of God to the little that was available, He supernaturally caused it to prosper. The moment Jesus exposed the natural realm to the heavenly realm there was instant supernatural multiplication.

When you and I expose what we have to an open heaven, there will be instant supernatural multiplication. How did Jesus do this? He lifted His hands in praise to the Father. I don't care what your bank account looks like or what your salary is, if you bring what you have to God, lift your hands in praise and thanksgiving to Him, you too will experience supernatural multiplication. We know that the food ended up being more than enough to feed thousands, with left-over baskets. Wow, what a blessing!

YOU ARE A VESSEL OF BLESSING

In all that we have examined from Matthew 14, there is a very simple principle that we often tend to overlook. *Give ye them to eat!* The key to experiencing the supernatural financial favor of God is our willingness to be a vessel of blessing. What do I mean by this term? So many times we are so absorbed with what we perceive to be our need, that we are not in a position (mentally, emotionally, or physically) to bless someone else. The disciples wanted to send the people away. What was the implication in that statement? They were basically telling Jesus, "We only have enough to manage our own needs!"

There is something that God taught me in my years of ministry—whatever He can get through you, He can get to you! The key is availing ourselves to Him as vessels of His supernatural provision. Do you know why so many Christians experience lack? They are selfish! As a result of this selfishness, they become habitual "seed eaters." The disciples did not realize that their fish lunch was simply a seed from which God wanted to produce a harvest that would meet the needs of thousands.

You may be in a situation right now, and you are saying, "I don't have enough!" That's because what you have in your hand is not for your need, it is simply a seed. Do not eat your seed! If the disciples would have eaten that meal instead of bringing it to Jesus, they would not have been filled. The Bible says that they were filled and they had baskets of food left over. That is what the favor of God can do! Remember, the favor of God is a covenant right. It will satisfy you beyond your capacity to receive. So instead of trying to figure out how and why, ask God, who and what: "Lord who do you want me to bless with what I have?" "What do you want me to do with the seed in my hand?"

> *The spirit of poverty always causes a person to do two things: blame their circumstance for their lack, and feel entitled.*

I know that this may seem strange to you, but I have found that it is the key to empowering yourself and breaking the bondage of the victim mentality. The spirit of poverty always causes a person to do two things: blame their circumstance for their lack, and feel entitled. The disciples felt entitled because they perceived themselves as lacking something; when the truth was they had more than enough, because they had Jesus Christ. When you realize that it is the divine will of your heavenly Father for you to prosper, and that the supernatural favor of God is operative in your life, you can never be a victim again! You are already blessed of your heavenly Father.

Every financial opposition will become a financial opportunity. What seems like oblivion will become an obligation to praise God. This is the key to experiencing financial favor. There was a time in my ministry when the church I was pastoring did not bring in a consistent income due to its size. The church was only a few months old, and still in it's developmental phase. This was a difficult time for my wife and me, being that we were in full-time ministry with two very young children, and not drawing a real salary from the church. I, like the disciples began to look to our circumstances for some sense of affirmation. This was a very disappointing exercise. The more I began to look to our congregation to help meet the financial obligations of my family, the worse things became. It got to the point where we were behind on many of our bills and we even felt discouraged about continuing in ministry. Somehow I had bought into the idea that struggling financially was normal for a pastor.

I subconsciously became a victim of my circumstances and thus felt entitled. God began to deal with me. He spoke to me through a man of God who said, "Your congregation is not your source." I said, "Really?" That was the first time I ever heard something like that. Even though I considered myself a man of faith I was still looking to man to meet my needs. The idea that God's favor could work in my life, regardless of what people around me were doing, was revolutionary.

God began to deal with my heart. I realized that this victim mentality had produced a selfish and self-centered attitude; and as a result, it brought barrenness into my life. I was waiting for someone to bless me, when in fact God was trying to teach me how to be a blessing. God's provision is not based on the size of your congregation.

As I began to pray and seek the Lord more, my wife and I began to receive revelation about supernatural provision. Everywhere we turned we heard about God being our supernatural provider. We began to share this teaching with our congregation. We were so excited. Two days later, one of our congregants came to our house with a money order for a thousand dollars. This was completely unsolicited and unexpected. This produced a ripple effect in the spiritual atmosphere of our lives. God was teaching us that His favor works. We started to see God's supernatural provision everywhere we turned. The more I thought about the favor of God, the more favor I saw being manifested and the more I became dissatisfied with the lack in our lives.

I began to declare the Word of God over our circumstances; I thanked God audibly for His supernatural favor and provision. I began to tell the devil to let our money go in the name of Jesus. I went outside and laid hands on our mailbox and said, "From this day forward I command you to be a divine receptacle of God's supernatural favor and provision. I dispatch the angels to go and retrieve the resources we need." The same day, I received another check in the mail for $500, the next day another $500; by the end of two weeks, we had received over $4,000 dollars (mostly from anonymous donors). Through those circumstances, God taught me that there is so much more than meets the natural eye when it comes to His favor. Since that time we have consistently experienced a deluge of financial blessings, including; thousands of dollars in debt miraculously canceled, countless financial miracles, and continual promotion and increase in our ministry. This favor is not exclusive only to my family; God wants to do the same thing for you today. We have access to heaven's blessing on a consistent basis once we align ourselves with heaven's agenda, and heaven's agenda is for you and me to be supernatural vessels of God's blessing and provision.

OUR HEAVENLY ACCOUNT

Not because I desire a gift: but I desire fruit that may abound to your account (Philippians 4:17).

We have seen thus far that we serve an amazing God! This truth is mind-blowing! Our Lord demonstrated to us the power that supernatural favor has to meet us at the very point of our need, even in the midst of an impossible circumstance. Jesus took the little that the disciples had and multiplied it. How was this able to take place? It is great to know that Jesus could do it, but can it work for us?

I believe there is a key to experiencing heaven's financial favor, and that key is understanding that the invisible realm is more real than the physical realm. Jesus lifted up the natural resources that were given to Him to heaven and thanked His Father. Why did He do this? Paul the apostle, writing to the church at Philippi, reveals a very interesting concept. In Philippians 4, Paul addresses the church concerning their financial offering to him. This church sent resources to meet his financial need in the past, and he is calling on their assistance again. In the 17th verse, Paul says, "Not because I desire a gift: but I desire fruit that may abound to your account." What is Paul talking about? He is referring to our heavenly account. Paul explains that the church in Philippi has a heavenly account, and every time they sow into God's work and meet someone's physical need, there is a credit that is issued in the spiritual realm.

> *I believe there is a key to experiencing heaven's financial favor, and that key is understanding that the invisible realm is more real than the physical realm.*

Just like we have a physical bank account in the natural where we can make deposits and withdrawals; we also have an account in heaven that we can withdraw from when we need it. Many people do not understand this truth. Every act of obedience, every seed sown, and every word spoken is making a deposit into your heavenly account. The word account here is the Greek word *logos* (Strong's, G3056), which means a word or to speak. The implication is that this heavenly account is voice activated. We make withdrawals from this account by speaking faith-filled words. This is why Jesus lifted up the bread to heaven and said, "Thank you!" He was making a withdrawal from His heavenly account. It did not matter what the situation looked like in the natural, His heavenly account was full of divine resources.

You and I have access to the same heavenly resources. In fact, I remember driving down the street one day and the Holy Spirit began to speak to me. He said, "Faith is the currency of the Kingdom!" I remember asking God to clarify what He meant by this statement. As I meditated on this truth, God began to unveil the revelation behind it. I began to see that we have a heavenly account that is more real than our physical bank account. When we are trying to purchase something in the natural, we make a withdrawal from our bank account. In the same manner, when we have a financial need we can access heaven's storehouse. How do we access heaven's storehouse? We must open up our mouths and speak. When we speak faith-filled words and act on them, we are placing a demand on the unseen realm.

The more we obey the Word of God, the more fruit "abounds to our account." This is why Paul said in Philippians 4:19, "My God shall supply all your need, according to His riches in glory by Christ Jesus." He did not say, "According to your bank account balance." It doesn't matter what things look like in the natural realm, financial favor is supplied by the repository of heaven. The more we are conscious of this revelation, the more we will experience its positive effects in our lives. Many people's heavenly account is empty because their outlook is confined to the natural realm. This is why they don't sow or seek to meet the needs of others. They are spiritual hoarders! Whenever we hoard to ourselves, we experience barrenness.

I don't know about you, but I want to experience God's riches in glory. I believe that when Jesus prayed and blessed the bread and fish, the glory of God descended. The glory of God has the ability to accelerate and multiply. Everything that God does in our lives is according to His riches, and heaven's bank can never go bankrupt. I remember a time when my wife and I desperately needed a vehicle. We just had our second child and the current vehicle we were driving did not have enough room. My wife and I began to pray. Once we agreed in faith that we were ready to receive a vehicle, we started to speak it forth. For weeks I would thank God for the specific make and model that we wanted. I acted as one who had already received.

We began making deposits into our heavenly account, even though our physical budget could not support another vehicle. Out of the blue, we received all the money we needed to buy our vehicle; it was paid in full! Glory be to God! Where did this money come from? It came from our account in heaven! All we did was make a withdrawal.

> *The glory of God has the ability to accelerate and multiply. Everything that God does in our lives is according to His riches, and heaven's bank can never go bankrupt.*

This is what the favor of God on our lives can do. You and I have to learn to access this supernatural favor on a consistent basis.

FAVOR DECLARATION

Father, in the name of Jesus, I thank You for who You are and all that You have done. Right now I decree and declare that my finances are in perfect alignment with the Word of God. I thank You, Lord, that in accordance with Second Corinthians 9:8, that You are able to make all grace abound toward me, that I having all sufficiency in all things abound to every good work. Deuteronomy 8:18 states that it is God who gives you the power to get wealth, that you may establish His covenant. I thank You, Lord, that I have the power to get wealth. I thank You that it will be used for the purposes of establishing Your covenant. I have more than enough in Jesus' name. All of my needs are met and I lack nothing. I am blessed to be a blessing. I am a giver, and I can be trusted as a good steward of both material and spiritual resources. I am not selfish with what You give me, but I will use what You give me to establish Your kingdom on earth. Your favor infuses all of my efforts and endeavors. I am not deficient financially. My income is not limited but unlimited. I am disciplined in financial matters. My mind and my spirit self are receptive to witty inventions. I command the mountain of lack (any and all forms) to be removed from my life. I take authority over the spirit of poverty, and I command it to leave every area of my life. I take dominion over the devourer and his devices in operation in every area of my financial life. I am prosperous in every area in accordance with Psalm 1. These things I declare in Jesus' name! Amen.

Chapter 8

Unlimited Favor

Now unto Him that is able to do exceeding
abundantly above all that we ask or think, according
to the power that worketh in us (Ephesians 3:20).

THERE IS A SPIRITUAL TRUTH THAT ALL OF US NEED TO EMBRACE;
the supernatural favor of God is absolutely unlimited in it its
demonstration. We have consistently seen throughout the Word of
God that God's favor is our birthright. Just as the favor of God rested
on Abraham every day of his life, this same supernatural favor has

come on us who believe in the Lord Jesus Christ. The issue is that of faith and confidence. Do you really believe that God can do anything?

The Bible says in the book of Ephesians chapter 3, verse 20, "Now unto Him that is able to do exceeding abundantly above all that we ask or think, according to the power that worketh in us." Notice that it says God is able to do "exceeding abundantly." There is a place in God called "exceeding abundantly." The word exceeding literally means far beyond. The power of God's supernatural favor goes far beyond our level of comprehension. As a matter of fact, if you can imagine the greatest blessing in the world, what God has for us goes far beyond that! The Bible says that it is far above anything that we can ask or think. Do you realize who the God that you serve really is?

Religion has taught us to put limitations on God's power. To be quite honest, I believe that our thinking has a tendency to be too small. I declare that the body of Christ is entering into a season of "exceeding abundantly"! This means that you and I are going to begin to take God at His Word. We know that He is El Shaddai (More Than Enough), but do we really believe that His power is limitless? Isn't it funny how we can go to church on Sunday (or Saturday) and sing songs declaring the awesomeness of God, and go home filled with worry and fear? If God is so awesome and the favor of God is so supernatural, why don't we experience this on a daily basis?

Well, we have to read the last part of that same verse, "according to the power that worketh in us." What does this mean? This means that God is able to manifest His supernatural to the degree that His power is at work inside us. The word for power is the Greek word *dynamis* (Strong's, G1411) and it means the power inherent in something by virtue of its nature. It is where we derive the English word dynamite. This power that Paul is referring to is the explosive, miracle-working power of God. The word for work is the Greek word *energeo* (Strong's, G1754), and it means to be operative or effective. It's where we get the English word energy. So we can say, the miracle-working power of God's grace can only manifest to the degree that this power is first operating inside us. It is like holding a stick of dynamite. In order to see the power of that dynamite demonstrated, there must first be something (usually a fire) that ignites the dynamite from the inside. This ignition triggers the explosion. Without being ignited, there will be no explosion. Once the match is lit and the dynamite is set ablaze, the latent power within that dynamite will be released, and everyone will see its power.

> **The more the Word of God is operating inside us, the more we will expect from God.**

In the same way, until you and I are ignited with the *energeo* of God from the inside, we will not be able to see that power manifest in our lives. I believe that this ignition switch is called *expectation*. In order to see the power of God manifested in greater measure, we must first increase our level of expectation. How do we increase our level of expectation? By meditating on the Word of God. The more the Word of God is operating inside us, the more we will expect from God. The more we expect God to do, the more He does! His Word is like a trigger that produces expectation inside our spirit. Remember, the attitude of expectation is the atmosphere for the miraculous. What do you expect God to do in your life today? Are you expecting to see His goodness and favor at every turn? Are you excited about the favorable report that you are going to hear today? If not, then you need to change your expectation.

If hope is the confident expectation of good, then doubt is the confident expectation of bad. God's power will only work in your life according to your level of expectation and anticipation. Some might say, "I don't believe that!" Of course, and that is exactly why they are not seeing the favor of God manifested in their lives. This reminds me of a conversation that I had with someone one day. I was walking through my office and someone said, "How are you doing?" I replied, "I'm blessed and highly favored!" The person became upset with my statement and said that I was putting myself at a higher level than them. The reality is that I was at a higher level, because I had a higher level of expectation.

Your level of expectation always determines your level of manifestation. Your attitude determines your altitude! I have been in meetings where there was a word given about being blessed, and some people get extremely excited and hopeful, while others become cynical. You probably figured out who the recipients of the blessings were—those who awaited God's promise with great anticipation. People who expect always get blessed.

WHAT'S IN *YOUR* HOUSE?

Now there cried a certain woman of the wives of the sons of the prophets unto Elisha, saying, Thy servant my husband is dead; and thou knowest that thy servant did fear the LORD: and the creditor is come to take unto him my two sons to be bondmen. And Elisha said unto her, What shall I do for thee? tell me, what hast thou in the house? And she said, Thine handmaid hath not any thing in the house, save a pot of oil. Then he said, Go, borrow thee vessels abroad of all thy neighbours, even empty vessels; borrow not a few. And when thou art come in, thou shalt shut the door upon thee and upon thy sons, and shalt pour out into all those vessels, and thou shalt set aside that which is full. So she went from him, and shut the door upon her and upon her sons, who brought the vessels to her; and she poured out. And it came to pass, when the vessels were full, that she said unto her son, Bring me yet a vessel. And he said unto her, There is not a vessel more. And the oil stayed (2 Kings 4:1-6).

In the book of Second Kings chapter 4 we see a powerful story, which I believe masterfully illustrates the unlimited power of the favor of God. The centerpiece is not the profoundness of the prophet Elisha, but the desperate situation of this widow woman. She was in a position where creditors were about to take her sons and there seemed to be no solution in the natural realm. I believe that God allowed this to be written just to prove to us that there is no situation that He cannot handle. She wondered if there was anything that the prophet could do for her. This woman found favor in the eyes of the prophet Elisha. You must understand that it was a huge deal to encounter the favorable treatment of a man of God in those days. He asked her if there was anything that he could do for her. As you can imagine, she quickly told the man of God the situation. Instead of receiving a list of public aid organizations or wealthy business people in the area, he asked a very simple yet profound question, "What's in the house?" Why did Elisha ask the woman this question? This situation qualified as an opportunity to see the supernatural favor of God in action.

It was discussed previously that the favor of God is an empowerment and an accelerator. If you are a covenant child of God, you already have everything necessary to meet what you perceive to be an immediate need or a desperate situation. You are already blessed! The woman answered the man of God in the same way that many of us would answer, she said, "I don't have anything, except a pot of oil." She never considered that the oil in her house could even remotely come close to meeting her need. She was in a situation where what she had seemed extremely insufficient, but the favor of God was supernaturally transferred to the little that she had.

The man of God did not empathize with the widow woman for one second. The first thing he told the woman to do was to *"Go"!* The word used for go is the Hebrew word *yalak* (Strong's, H3212). This word means to proceed or to walk on. So Elisha was telling the woman that her limitation was not an excuse to stop moving forward in the miracle that she was expecting from God.

Never halt in your expectation. Don't stop believing God! Keep moving forward and you will see the favor of God manifest like never before. The woman was commanded to go and borrow empty pots from her neighbor as many as possible. He told her to shut the door behind her and her sons, then pour the oil into the vessels and set them aside once she was done. Every time the vessel became full she would tell her sons to fetch more vessels. The more vessels she received, the more oil poured out. It finally came to the point where they ran out of vessels and the oil stayed.

When she told the man of God what happened, he told her to sell the oil, pay the debt, and live off the rest. This is a powerful revelation! The more she brought empty vessels, the more they were filled. The vessels represent expectation. The implication of the text is that if she would have continued bringing vessels, the oil would have continued to pour out. There was a limitless supply. The only thing that caused the oil to stop flowing was a lack of vessels to contain it.

> *Never halt in your expectation. Don't stop believing God! Keep moving forward and you will see the favor of God manifest like never before.*

This tells us that God is willing to pour out as much favor as we are willing to receive. The more we expect, the more we will receive; regardless of circumstances. The woman did not realize that there was a limitless flow right in her house. I am here to tell you that the *favor of God* can bring increase, multiplication, acceleration, debt cancelation, restoration, healing, and blessing. It is more precious than gold or exotic stones. It can buy goods without money or price. It all depends on your level of expectation.

The problem that the woman had was not limited resources, but limited expectation. She was confined to the natural. I believe that the reason the prophet Elisha told the woman to shut the door is because he was trying to get her to build her expectation. He didn't want her to be distracted by the circumstances around her. He didn't want her to look at or listen to people; she was only to obey the Word of God. God said *"Go,"* and she went.

God is telling you to do the same thing! He is saying *"Go"!* You are thinking, *But God, I don't have enough money...or education!* But God, like the prophet Elisha, is asking you, "What's in your house?" The house represents your heart. What's in your heart is the real issue. Do you have a house (heart) full of expectation? Do you believe that God can do anything? If you do, then that is all you need to experience the unlimited favor of God. It doesn't matter what your education level is or your financial status. This favor isn't fair! If it can work for a widow woman in the Old Testament, then surely it can work for the born-again child of God who is a seed of Abraham. What's in your house?

A Testimony of Favor

Several years ago, my wife and I were newly married and I had recently lost my job. What were my wife and I going to do? On top of the fact that I was no longer employed, my wife was several months pregnant. Difficult situations are simply qualifiers for God's miraculous power. This situation definitely qualified us to receive a miracle. I applied to several places of employment to no avail. As we began to pray, God told us to do the most illogical thing I could imagine; sow a seed. Sow a seed? Yes! Everywhere we went God began to lay it on our hearts to minister to people's needs.

One particular day stood out when God told us to give the last that we had to a single mother at our church. We did it! She was so blessed by it that she came to us afterward and thanked us. Little did we know that seed was simply a key that God would use to unlock His favor and blessing in our lives. As we sowed in faith, it set off a chain reaction of blessing. People began to come up to us everywhere and tell us that God told them to give us something. Our landlord came to us and told me that God wanted him to give me something; it was $200 in .cash. (This was before we paid a single deposit or first months rent). Amazing! When was the last time your landlord gave you cash? Every day there was another blessing.

Another interesting phenomenon was the supernatural multiplication of our resources. Twenty dollars would spend like $100 and $50 would spend like $200. It was amazing! During this time my wife and I were believing that God would manifest even more finances. My wife went to her school to see if she could possibly get an internship. As she was speaking with one of her friends in the graduate studies department, she told her that she had been on her mind. She said that she wanted to award my wife and me a $4,500 contract from a special grant that had been created. Wow!

There was one miraculous manifestation of God's favor after another. During this time of unemployment, every bill that we had was paid supernaturally. On top of all of this, the following year, my wife and I made six figures. Thank you Jesus! God took us from the pit to the palace. We went from unemployment to more than enough. Can you believe this? I can, because it happened to me! All it took was one act of faith coupled with expectation to release an unlimited supply of heaven's rain. The thing is, God is no respecter of persons. If He did it for us, He will do it for you. All you have to do is bring your vessels of expectation to Him and He will fill them every single time. Expect!

A TESTIMONY OF FAVOR

There was a woman we know who had been attempting to come to the United States for several years. Three of her siblings and her stepfather all lived in the U.S. When her youngest sister was graduating from college, she attempted to come and visit, but her visa application was denied. On another occasion, during a time before her sister's wedding and after being selected as the maid of honor, her visa application was also denied. On yet another occasion, she wanted to attend her youngest brother's wedding, and her visa application was denied again. After waiting in line for hours and calling around to everyone she knew to gather documents for the embassy, she was still coldly denied. In the country where she lives, it is very difficult to get a visa to the United States. Even though her mother works as a high-ranking official of the law, she was still unable to secure her visa.

About a year ago, she attempted to get her visa to attend her brother's wedding and she solicited our prayers (she is my sister-in-law by the way). We began to ask God to release His favor, goodness, and wisdom in this situation. As we prayed that prayer over her, she began to move forward in her pursuit of her visa. As she arrived at the embassy for the third time, she was met with the most interesting scenario. As she sat before the interviewer, before she could even show him her paperwork, she was told to come back the next day. When she arrived the next day, she was issued a two-year visa. Praise the Lord! Notice that she did not allow her expectation to diminish. She continued to expect the miraculous to take place. Like the widow woman in the book of Kings, the favor of God was poured into the container of her expectation.

> *There is no situation or circumstance that the grace of God cannot handle.*

I am here to tell you that the favor of God will accomplish the miraculous in your life. It will do what no person can do! It will purchase what no amount of money can buy. All we have to do is to expect it to manifest. My sister-in-law went to the embassy again even though she was previously denied and there seemed to be no hope in the natural. The favor of God caused her to experience preferential treatment. She was picked out of a crowd! She did not need to go to an outside source to receive her miracle; everything she needed was in her house. All she needed to do was to place an expectation on God's supernatural favor; and when she did, there was an almost immediate manifestation. You see, God's favor is unlimited. There is no situation or circumstance that the grace of God cannot handle.

FAVOR DECLARATION

Father, I thank You for Your unlimited power toward me as I believe. I declare that Your power at work in me is unlimited and therefore your exceeding abundant ability is manifested in my life. I declare that even as I fill my heart with expectation, I will see your goodness. I declare that every need, difficulty, or circumstance in my life is simply an opportunity for You to display Your power and goodness. I thank You that Your favor in my life is unlimited, in Jesus' name. Amen!

Chapter 9

ON THE EDGE OF
THE BLESSING

*And Moses said unto the people, Fear ye not,
stand still, and see the salvation of the LORD,
which He will shew to you to day: for the
Egyptians whom ye have seen to day, ye shall see
them again no more for ever* (Exodus 14:13).

M Y FATHER WAS A SELF-PROCLAIMED EXPERT FISHERMAN. HE
believed that he was even better than Roland Martin (a
famous fisherman). When I was a young boy, my father would take

me to South Georgia to go fishing in the famous Jackson Lake. The lake was behind a dam, and this was where some of the best fish were located. In order to access this area of the lake, it was necessary to climb an 8-foot wall that was above one of the deepest points of the lake. I found this experience horrifying. In order to get the best results we had to get close to the edge of the wall. I was not an experienced swimmer, and the thought of coming that close to the edge was very frightening.

My father, on the other hand, saw things from a different vantage point. Due to his love of fish and fishing, he was willing to make certain sacrifices to achieve the best results. To him, it was not a matter of standing on a dangerous ledge, it was a matter of standing on the edge of his blessing.

In the book of Exodus, the Israelites found themselves in a similar predicament; they were between Pharaoh's army and the Red Sea. Prior to this situation, they experienced the miraculous hand of God in bringing them out of Egyptian bondage. Now they found themselves being pursued by Pharaoh himself and six hundred of his chariots. What were they going to do? Well, most of them did what they were accustomed to doing; they complained. Why did they complain? They complained because they were terrified by what seemed to be an impossible situation and a losing battle.

Have you ever been in a place like this? We have spoken extensively about the supernatural favor of God, but you may not be feeling very supernatural right now. You may be on the edge! I am here to tell you that you are standing on the edge, but it is not the edge of your defeat or your demise—you, my friend, are standing on the very edge of the blessing.

The children of Israel couldn't see that every promise that God made would absolutely come to pass. They were blinded by what they saw in the natural. If Pharaoh came any closer they (in their minds) would drown in the Red Sea. The danger was imminent! Many people can identify with this scenario. Unfortunately, many people do what they have always done; complain. Complaining is a favor neutralizer. No one likes a complainer, especially not God. Every time we engage in the exercise of murmuring and complaining, we step outside of a position of favor and blessing. Remember, our words release the favor of God in our lives. By the same token, our words can inhibit the favor of God from flowing the way God intends.

> *Every time we engage in the exercise of murmuring and complaining, we step outside of a position of favor and blessing.*

God was simply using this difficult situation to glorify Himself. God already made a covenant promise to Abraham 430 years prior that He would deliver his descendants with a strong hand and give them the land of promise. In other words, this could not possibly be the end, because God cannot break His promise. This was a temporary situation designed to push them closer to the promise of God. Exodus 14:13 says: "Fear ye not, stand still, and see the salvation of the Lord, which He will shew to you to day: for the Egyptians whom ye have seen to day, ye shall see them again no more for ever." The first thing that Moses instructed the people to do was to "Fear not"! Why did Moses tell the people to fear not? The first reason is that fear tends to be our first response in the natural. Most of us have conditioned ourselves to look at what we can see. The favor of God on your life is a spiritual reality that holds true regardless of what you can or cannot see.

The other reason Moses told the people to fear not is because fear is a favor inhibiter. Remember, the supernatural favor of God is activated by faith, and fear is the opposite of faith. The more we worry, complain, stress, and become anxious, the less we will see the favor of God manifest in our lives. Moses was telling them, "I know you are on the edge, but you are exactly were God wants you to be." Sometimes God brings us to the edge, because the edge symbolizes the end of ourselves, and that is exactly where the favor of God is located. As a matter of fact, the Bible says that God resists the proud, but gives grace (supernatural favor) to the humble (see James 4:6). The more we come to the end of ourselves in the midst of difficult circumstances, the more the favor of God will be revealed.

STAND STILL

After Moses told the people to refrain from fear, the very next imperative that was issued was to "Stand still." What does it mean to stand still? The phrase stand still is derived from the Hebrew word *yatsab* (Strong's, H3320) and it literally means to station oneself. It implies to stay firm or to keep your balance. To put it another way, in the midst of challenges and difficult circumstances, instead of allowing fear, worry, and dread to take control; we are instructed to station ourselves in the promises of God and the favor of God. Don't move out of the place of faith and expectation, because the place of faith and expectation is the position of favor. It is like waiting at the train station; if you want to catch the train, you must patiently await its arrival. It doesn't matter what things look like or how you feel, the train is on its way.

There is a train of supernatural favor on its way to your location, but you have to station yourself long enough to see it arrive. This requires spiritual discipline. I can't tell you the countless times I seemed to be standing on the edge of my breakthrough and did not even realize it. The thing that is so funny about God is that He does not respond to our emotional outbursts, He only responds to His Word. This is why we find it hard to stand still, because we have been trained to respond to our emotions. The problem is that God's favor is not an emotional response to your desperate situation, it is a spiritual reality based on the finished work of Christ. The more you and I learn to tap into this favor by faith, the more we will experience its divine benefits.

> *The problem is that God's favor is not an emotional response to your desperate situation, it is a spiritual reality based on the finished work of Christ.*

God was trying to remind the children of Israel that He had a covenant with them, and this covenant was that of supernatural favor and blessing. All they really needed to do was stand in this truth. God has a covenant with you through Jesus, and you need to stand in this truth as well. Why did God tell the children of Israel to stand still? The answer is found in Psalm 5:12,

> *For thou, LORD, wilt bless the righteous; with **favour** wilt thou compass him as with a shield.*

The reason God wanted them to stand still is because they were compassed about with favor; supernatural favor. What does it mean to be compassed with favor? The word compass is the Hebrew word *atar* (Strong's, H5849) and it means to surround or to crown. When you combine these two ideas what you will find is that the Israelites were surrounded with a crown of favor. Can you imagine this? The crown of favor that God placed on them was so large that it literally became a wall of divine protection and blessing around them. They couldn't see this crown because it is invisible to the natural eye. This is why God wanted them to be still, because they were already surrounded with His supernatural favor and blessing.

You and I have the same crown of favor on our lives. We are surrounded by a supernatural wall. This crown of favor shields us from the elements of the world and the attacks of the enemy. It is a crown of empowerment and grace. I remember experiencing this crown in my personal life. One night I was outside looking at the stars, and as I looked to the right, I saw a large halo around the moon. This halo was probably thousands of miles in circumference. I had never seen anything like this in my entire life. I asked God, "What is that?" The Lord spoke to me and said, "That is my crown of favor!" I noticed that I was in the very center of this crown. I realized that as long as I was in this place I would experience all that God made available to me.

Pharaoh represents satan. He is a spiritual antagonist, and his main goal is to move us from a position of favor to a position of fear. He attempts to accomplish this mission through intimidation and manipulation. He tells you that you will never make it past the trial that you're in. He tries to convince you that this is the end of the line. None of these things are true. In fact, you are so surrounded that the enemy can't even touch you. The devil only has power if you step out of position. As a matter of fact, the Hebrew word for shield is the word *tsinnah* (Strong's, H6793) and it means piercing barb. This is literally referring to a barbed wire or fence. The favor of God is like a barbed wire fence that keeps the enemy out!

If only the body of Christ would realize that the favor of God surrounds us like a shield. We are compassed with supernatural power, grace, ability, protection, and divine blessing. You are not helpless or defenseless, you are empowered. The Israelites didn't know that there was supernatural barbed wire surrounding them. All they saw was a terrifying pharaoh and six hundred chariots. The key to standing still is making up in your mind that what you know to be true spiritually is more real than what you see in the natural. Open up your mouth and declare that you are surrounded with the favor of God as with a shield. Declare that you are protected by God's power. It does not matter how bad things look, you are already blessed and you have a covenant right to the favor of God in your life.

SEE THE SALVATION OF THE LORD

The last thing that Moses instructed the children of Israel to do was to "See the salvation of the Lord." Notice that God did not say, experience the salvation of the Lord. They were going to experience it, but before they could experience it they had to see it. Why? In the kingdom of God believing is seeing. In the world system we have been trained to believe what we can see. We must retrain our minds to think according to the Word of God. Remember, standing still requires spiritual discipline. The real spiritual discipline is learning to see things through the eyes of faith. Are you saying that faith has eyes? Absolutely! Just as in the natural realm a child develops a sense of sight, in the spiritual realm we have to develop our spiritual sense of sight. How do we develop a sense of sight in the spiritual realm? We must refuse to look at what we see! The Bible says in Second Corinthians 4:18:

> *While we look not at the things which are seen, but at the things which are not seen: for the things which are seen are temporal; but the things which are not seen are eternal.*

What does this Scripture verse mean? Well, the word look is the Greek word *skopeo* (Strong's, G4648) and it means to fix one's eyes upon, or direct one's attention to. It is where we get the English word scope. A scope is a device that allows you to focus your eyes on something and make it bigger. The Bible says that we do not fix our eyes upon what we can see in the natural, but we must fix our eyes on the unseen. In many ways, this is a logical contradiction. How can you focus your eyes on something that is unseen? When the Bible talks about the unseen it is not talking about the nonexistent, it is talking about the invisible realm. It is referring to the supernatural!

> *The real spiritual discipline is learning to see things through the eyes of faith.*

If you want to see something that is difficult to see or distant in the natural, you must use a telescope. There are telescopes that are so powerful that human beings are able to see stars that are light years away. These stars are present, but they are not visible to the natural eye. When the Bible talks about seeing, it is talking about our ability to discern. This is an issue of spiritual discernment. So we can say, faith is the telescope of the spiritual realm. It gives us the ability to focus our spiritual eyes on the supernatural. The Bible says that the things which are seen are temporal or temporary, but the unseen things are eternal. In order to fix our eyes on the unseen, we have to use the telescope of faith. This is what the Bible was referring to in the book of Exodus. God was telling them to use the telescope of faith to see His salvation. God did not want them to regard Pharaoh and his army, because they were temporary. There was an eternal reality that superseded what they were observing in the natural.

If we are going to experience the supernatural favor of God, we must learn to fix our eyes and focus our attention on the truth of God's Word. Do not regard what you see in the physical! Whatever we look at we will gravitate toward. When you look at the physical, you will inevitably gravitate toward the physical. When we focus our attention on our circumstances, it produces fear, worry, and anxiety. However, if you make a quality decision to only look at the supernatural, you will gravitate toward the supernatural, and the supernatural will gravitate toward you. You will be filled with faith and expectation. I don't know what you are facing today, but if you will simply stand in a position of faith and expectation, and set your eyes on the Word of God, you will see the salvation of God manifest in your life.

> *If we are going to experience the supernatural favor of God, we must learn to fix our eyes and focus our attention on the truth of God's Word.*

A TESTIMONY OF FAVOR

During my first year of college, I tried my best to concentrate on enjoying my educational experience, but my financial concerns were always before my face. Toward the end of my first semester, I received a letter from the financial aid office telling me that the tuition aid I was expected to receive did not process, and I was responsible for a balance of $5,000 to continue my college education. I was devastated. I felt like Pharaoh's army was pursuing after me, and I was about to drown into a financial Red Sea. To you, $5,000 may not seem like much, but at the time it appeared to be a mountain. My parents were not wealthy and they had financial difficulties of their own. The only thing I knew to do at that time was to pray. A Christian friend of mine heard about my situation and said to me, "I'm glad I'm not you!" What a faith killer! Sometimes church people can be worse than the devil. Thankfully for me, I was not a quitter. I began to remind God of His promises. I declared that the favor of God surrounded me and that I had more than enough. The more I spoke faith, the worse the situation seemed.

Finally, I received a letter under my dorm room door stating that if I did not pay my balance in 24 hours, I was going to have all of my clothing and furniture thrown outside the dorm. Oh my God! What was I going to do? At this point, I booked an interview with the vice president of student services. His office was packed full of people who probably had the same sob story I had; some even worse. I began to pray in the Spirit. I started to thank God for His favor in this situation. There was a stirring inside my spirit that this situation was going to turn out for my good.

Every Scripture I knew on the favor of God came to the forefront of my mind. When it was my turn to meet with the vice president, he looked at my file and said that I needed to come up with the money or I would not be able to complete my education. All I could say was, "Sir, I cannot leave this school, I'm supposed to be here!" He looked at me with the most peculiar visage. I repeated that statement again and again. He told me that I needed to leave his office and that there was nothing that he could do for me. After I heard this, I called my mother on his phone. While I had her on the phone, I told him to speak to her (she was a woman of God). He reluctantly spoke to her and said, "Ma'am, there is nothing I can do for your son."

There was a brief silence. Then he looked at me and said I had an additional 24 hours to come up with the money. I was on the edge. This was a decision-making moment. Would I trust God or would I cave in to my feelings? The voice of the Lord came to me and said, "Trust Me!" The only thing to do at that point was to stand still and see His salvation be revealed. I worshiped and praised God with all my might. I sung so loudly my roommate became frustrated. Then the most remarkable thing happened—all the fear, worry, and anxiety went away. I felt as though I was surrounded by a tangible force; now I know it was the favor of God. The next morning on my way to class, I received a call from my brother-in-law. He told me to meet him downstairs in front of my dorm. When I met him, he opened his hand and pulled out a piece of notebook paper. As I unwrapped the paper, there was a check inside for $5,000. Hallelujah to the Lamb of God! I ran to the financial aid office shouting. I saw the manifestation of God's favor as I stood still on the edge of the blessing! God wants to do this for us each and every day. Will you receive your miracle today? The favor of God surrounds you like a shield!

FAVOR DECLARATION

Lord, I thank You that You are faithful to deliver me in every situation. I declare that just as Your Word says in Psalm 5:12, Your favor surrounds me as a shield and a crown. I declare that in every circumstance I stand still and I see Your salvation. I declare that I am not led by fear, my natural eyes, or even my emotions, but I am led only by the spoken word of God. In Jesus' name. Amen!

Chapter 10

SOUL PROSPERITY

*Beloved, I wish above all things that thou
mayest prosper and be in health, even as
thy soul prospereth* (3 John 1:2).

WE HAVE CLEARLY SEEN THROUGH THE WORD OF GOD THAT
favor belongs to the born-again believer. We, like Abraham,
have access to this supernatural favor 24 hours a day, 365 days a year.
Don't you like the sound of that? Year after year of favor! Nonetheless, we discovered that the favor of God was much more than an

arbitrary occurrence; it is in fact our birthright. We have inherited the favor of God that was on Abraham, and on our Lord Jesus Christ.

There is another dimension to the favor of God that we don't often think about. God wants to prosper us! How do we walk in this divine prosperity and what does it have to do with the favor of God? In Genesis 13:2, the Bible says, "And Abram was very rich in cattle, in silver, and in gold." It was clear that the favor of God on Abraham's life caused him to prosper. Anyone who is against prosperity has clearly not read the Bible. Abraham was a man of abundant material wealth and resources. This abundance was a reality every day of the 175-plus years of Abraham's life. Wow! What a blessing!

The truth is that prosperity includes abundant financial provision, but it is so much more than that. The Word of God tells us throughout the book of Third John that it is the will of God for us to prosper. The question remains: how does this prosperity become a reality in our lives? I have been in meetings where I was told that if I simply sowed a seed, everything would be fine. There were many times when I gave money to different ministries and absolutely nothing happened. Why? Was the preacher lying? I personally believe that it has nothing to do with the preacher. In fact, the Bible tells us in Third John that we will prosper and be in health *as our soul prospers.* What does this mean? It simply means that prosperity begins inside us. Prosperity is from the inside out, not the outside in.

The word soul is derived from the Greek word *psyche* (*psuche*, Strong's, G5590) which means the seat of the feelings, desires, affections, and emotions. Simply put, our soul is the conglomerate of the mind, will, and emotions. It is where our decisions are made and our desires are carried out. The Jewish understanding goes even further than this. From a Jewish perspective, prosperity deals with wholeness.

It comes from the Hebrew word *shalom* (Strong's, H7965), which means peace. Therefore you and I can only walk in prosperity to the degree that we are whole on the inside—soul prosperity.

It is a spiritual law that what you meditate on you will ultimately manifest. The Bible says, "The thoughts of the diligent tend only to plenteousness; but of every one that is hasty only to want" (Proverbs 21:5). The thoughts of the diligent are only concerned with plenteousness. What is plenteousness? It means abundance or plenty. People who are diligent only see things from the vantage point of more than enough. They never concentrate on what they lack; as a result they only see abundance in their lives.

Contrariwise, the Bible says that all those who are hasty only concentrate on want or lack. What does it mean to be hasty? The concept of hastiness in Hebrew means to be pressed in or confined. It implies being mentally and emotionally imprisoned. It is kind of like being invited out to eat with no money and you are not sure whether the person who invited you will cover the check; the entire time you will be thinking about the bill. You will not be able to enjoy your food, because your mind is imprisoned to what you are lacking. This is what it means to be hasty, it is a mindset that is always focused on what it does not have. This kind of attitude actually produces more lack and barrenness in a person's life.

On the other hand, if we are diligent, we focus on the favor, goodness, and abundance of God, and that abundance is manifested in our lives. Never forget this spiritual truth; what you set your mind on, you will manifest! So we can see that our mentality can have a profound effect on our ability to walk in God's prosperity. It would be enough alone to highlight the relationship between prosperity and our mentality, but the Bible does not stop there. The soul includes mind, will, and emotions.

> *Never forget this spiritual truth; what you set your mind on, you will manifest!*

EMOTIONAL PROSPERITY

When I was in the corporate world, there was a phrase that was often used: emotional intelligence. The short definition of this phrase is the ability to control or manage one's emotions in a systematic way. I personally don't subscribe to the philosophy that a person can do such a thing apart from God, but I find the concept interesting. Researchers discovered that emotional health affects the overall health of companies and organizations. In the same way, the emotional well-being of a born-again believer directly affects their ability to flow in God's favor and prosperity.

There are so many Christians who are suffering from emotional turmoil and they are wondering why they are not able to prosper. Remember, prosperity begins inside us; every material blessing that we receive is affected by our level of wholeness within. If you are walking around bitter and resentful toward people, don't be surprised if that same bitterness and resentment creates a prison of lack and frustration. I can personally identify with this emotional state, because I suffered from bitterness for years. I was always angry at what I did not have and frustrated that I was going through the challenges that I seemed to be going through. I became negative and offensive. This negativity closed doors to many blessings in my life. Eventually, the Lord opened my eyes to this truth and I was set free.

Earlier, we talked about the fact that supernatural favor is released through the words that we speak. In the same way, our words have the power to create an atmosphere of ill favor around us. When we choose to be negative, we are in affect shutting the door of God's supernatural provision in our lives. Just like the children of Israel were always complaining in the wilderness, you and I can cause ourselves to go around the mountain of delay, stagnation, and lack when we don't make a decision to take control over our emotions with the Word of God. This is what John was referring to in his epistle to Gaius. Once our souls (mind, will, and emotions) are prospering, that prosperity will manifest in every other area of our lives as well.

As a pastor, I have come across countless people who are confined to a prison of negativity that they have built with their own hands. They blame everyone else for their difficulty. They often do not take responsibility for their choices. I remember talking to a missionary, and he told me that no one wanted to help him. He complained that he was not able to raise the kind of financial support he needed to accomplish the missionary work that God called him to do. The more I spoke with him, the more drained I became. What was the problem? He was hasty! In other words, his soul was not prospering. He made a decision to focus his energy on what he did not have, and who wasn't helping him, instead of concentrating on the goodness of God. He became a prisoner of unhealthy emotions. As he spoke, his words were saturated with offense and anger. This minister did not realize that he was being a favor repellent instead of a favor magnet. Why? True prosperity begins in our soul, not our bank account.

Remember, prosperity does not come from the outside—it comes from within. We have to *decide* to be joyous. We must *decide* to praise God no matter what it looks like in the natural. We have to *be grateful* for what God has already done for us. The more we do this, the more the prosperity of God will flood our soul, and the more this prosperity will overflow into our wallets. Bitterness always produces barrenness! The more bitter you are, the more barren you are. On the other hand, when you decide that you will live above all offense and love everyone; you will activate God's favor in a very powerful way. Will you choose to prosper in your soul today?

> *We have to be grateful for what God*
> *has already done for us.*

PROSPERITY THROUGH MEDITATION

*This book of the law shall not depart out of thy mouth; but thou shalt **meditate** therein **day and night,** that thou mayest observe to do according to all that is written therein: for then thou shalt make thy way prosperous, and then thou shalt have good success* (Joshua 1:8).

The question remains: how are you and I supposed to experience soul prosperity? The Word of God tells us exactly how to do it! We are to meditate on the Word of God. As a matter of fact, the Bible tells us in the book of Joshua 1:8 that we are to meditate on the Word of God day and night. When most people think of mediation, they visualize a monk with a shaved head kneeling down in front of some statue. This is not what the Bible is referring to at all. In fact, the Hebrew word for meditate is the word *hagah* (Strong's, H1897), and it means to moan, growl, mutter, or speak; usually repetitiously. God is telling us to speak His Word over and over to ourselves. This is biblical meditation. Jesus said that the words that He spoke were spirit and life. Hebrews 4:12 says:

> *For the word of God is quick, and powerful, and sharper than any twoedged sword, piercing even to the dividing asunder of soul and spirit, and of the joints and marrow, and is a discerner of the thoughts and intents of the heart.*

In other words, the word of God is life-giving and full of the miracle-working power of God. The more we meditate in the Word, the more the Word gets down inside us. If we do this day and night, with the intent to do what it says, we will make our way *prosperous*. This is a phenomenal promise! Notice it does not say that God will make our way prosperous; it says that we will make our own way prosperous. Why? God has already blessed us according to Ephesians chapter 1. We have to appropriate this blessing inside us by meditating in God's Word. When the Bible uses the word prosperity in Joshua 1:8, it is the word *tsalach* (Strong's, H6743), and it means to advance, to progress, or to succeed. Interestingly enough, the word for prosperity found in Third John is the word *euodoo* (Strong's, G2137); this word means to have a successful journey. Both of these words imply an assignment or purpose. We see that God has a divine purpose for His divine prosperity. God does not just prosper us so that we can look good; the prosperity that we have been given is to accomplish His specific assignment for our lives.

> *God does not just prosper us so that we can look good; the prosperity that we have been given is to accomplish His specific assignment for our lives.*

Simply put, you and I have a job to do, we have a journey to embark on, and we need supernatural as well as financial resources for this journey. When we speak the Word of God over and over again, we release the supernatural favor of God. You ought to try that right now! Say the following out loud:

> *God I praise You and thank You for Your unmerited favor in my life. I thank You that through Jesus Christ, I am blessed and empowered to prosper. I have more than enough. My heavenly bank account is full, and I abound with blessings. Thank You for the favor and resources necessary to fulfill Your assignment for my life. In Jesus' name! Amen!*

Don't you feel good after saying that? If you don't, you will; just keep saying it! Keep speaking the Word of God over yourself and over your children and you are going to manifest the supernatural favor and prosperity of God in your life. Remember, this is the same Word that created the universe. This is the same Word that was in the beginning, and this is the same Word that you are declaring out of your mouth right now. As you are confessing you are making your way more and more prosperous, and eventually you will end up in a place called *"Good Success."* This word simply means to have insight or comprehension. So God doesn't just want you to be blessed and highly favored, He wants you to teach others how to be blessed as well. What a marvelous God we serve!

FAVOR DECLARATION

Father, I thank You that it is Your desire for me to prosper and be in health as my soul prospers. I declare that my soul is filled with God's prosperity, and I prosper from the inside out. I declare that my soul is not contaminated by fear, bitterness, and unbelief. I declare, according to Joshua 1:8, that I will meditate on God's Word, I will make my way prosperous, and I will have good success! Amen!

Chapter 11

THINKING DIFFERENTLY

*I beseech you therefore, brethren, by the mercies of God, that ye present your bodies a living sacrifice, holy, acceptable unto God, which is your reasonable service. And be not conformed to this world: but be ye **transformed by the renewing of your mind**, that ye may prove what is that good, and acceptable, and perfect, will of God* (Romans 12:1-2).

ONE OF MY FAVORITE MOVIES IS A FILM CALLED *THE MATRIX*. In this movie, the main character, Neo, is taken to the character named Morpheus. While sitting in a room with Morpheus, Neo is told that the world that he has grown up in his entire life is simply an illusion. Neo is given the option to take a red pill or a blue pill. The red pill will allow him to experience the truth and the blue pill will insert him back into the artificial program which he has known his entire life. As you may have guessed, Neo opted for the red pill and so began his exciting journey into the truth.

This dialogue in *The Matrix* reminds me of many people in the body of Christ. God has given us the option to continue in our ignorance or to be enlightened with the truth of God's Word. Accepting the truth of God's Word requires something called mind renewal. Simply put, God wants us to think differently. As simple as this statement may seem, it is yet another key to unleashing God's supernatural favor in your life. In the book of Romans chapter 12, Apostle Paul writes to the church at Rome and encourages them to present their bodies as living sacrifices, and to not be conformed to this world system, but to be transformed by the renewing of their minds.

> *God has given us the option to continue in our ignorance or to be enlightened with the truth of God's Word.*

The Greek word for transformed is the word *morphoo* (Strong's, G3445), and it means to change shapes or take on a higher form. Interestingly enough, the name Morpheus is a play on this Greek word and it also means to transform. What does God mean when He says, "be transformed"? He is telling us to change into the shape of His original intent for our lives. In the context of supernatural favor, God wants us to change from a life governed by the natural, to a life governed by the supernatural. He does not want us to be controlled by what we see, but by the power of His Word.

How do we accomplish this task? He tells us exactly how in the second phrase of Romans 12 verse 2, "be ye transformed by the renewing of your mind." The Word of God tells us that you and I will experience this transformation by mind renewal. In other words, we are to access the supernatural favor, blessing, and power of God through thinking differently. This word is derived from the Greek word *anakainosis* (Strong's, G342), and it means to renovate or make new. In order to be transformed, you and I must renovate our thinking. I don't know about you, but for me it has been both challenging and rewarding to change my way of thinking. In fact, our way of thinking controls every aspect of our lives. The Bible says in Proverbs 23:7, "as he thinketh in his heart, so is he." If we change our thinking we can change our lives.

Earlier, I spoke about the fact that negativity is a favor neutralizer. The more we think negatively, the more we become disempowered. This way of thinking is what I call the poverty mentality. What is the poverty mentality? It is a way of thinking that is controlled by fear, scarcity, and lack. When we are operating in a poverty mentality we can never be thankful for what God has already done for us.

Let me give you an example of a poverty mindset at work. Let's say you are in a financial crisis; the poverty mentality immediately puts you in the posture of a victim. The poverty mindset says, "God, why is this happening to me?" Notice that the poverty way of thinking associates challenging circumstances as "something happening to me." On the other hand, the favor mentality says, "God, I thank You for another opportunity to see Your favor, goodness, and provision in action!" Do you see the difference? One is the attitude of a victim, the other is an attitude of a victor. When you realize that you are blessed by God, you can never take the posture of a victim again! Remember, God has already spoken well over us. We are already favored of our heavenly Father by virtue of Jesus Christ. We have to place a demand on this supernatural favor through faith and expectation; and in order to be able to do that, we have to think differently.

THE FAVOR PARADIGM

When the Bible deals with changing our thinking, it is not simply referring to a temporary alteration; it is talking about a supernatural paradigm shift. What do I mean by the term supernatural paradigm shift? First of all, I think it would help to define paradigm. A paradigm is a mental framework or worldview that underlies our thoughts and behaviors. This is a deeply rooted pattern of thinking that can have generational influence. For example, when I was a young boy, I was always told to turn the radio or television off during lightning storms. Though I never saw a television explode during a storm or anyone in my family for that matter; we developed a fear-based mindset from information that we were given. This is what is meant by a paradigm.

So when referring to a paradigm shift, I am talking about a complete shift, overhaul, and renovation of our core mindsets. This shift cannot take place on its own; there must be supernatural power available to act as the catalyst for this shift. That supernatural catalyst is the Word of God. The Word of God carries the miracle-working power of God, and it is that miracle-working power that we need to shift our thinking. In fact, you and I have to have a favor paradigm if we are going to experience the supernatural favor of God on a consistent basis.

> *The Word of God carries the miracle-working power of God, and it is that miracle-working power that we need to shift our thinking.*

The Bible says that we are to experience this supernatural transformation by the renewing or renovating of our minds. Imagine a construction worker renovating a house. In order to accomplish this task, the worker has to tear down old walls and remove outdated carpeting and wallpaper. This can be a very painful process to look at, but when it is complete, the house looks beautiful. Our mind is that house, and the Word of God is the construction worker. The more we meditate on the Word of God, the more the Word of God tears down old ways of thinking and erects new ones.

You may be someone who has had curses spoken over you your entire life. People may have told you that you won't succeed or that you will never achieve your dreams. I am here to tell you that satan is a liar. In fact, I was controlled by negative motivators most of my life. I wanted to prove to others that I would be successful one day. What I did not realize is that the moment I became born again, I became successful. I was born to succeed! If you have a relationship with God through Jesus Christ, you are born to succeed as well. You no longer have to walk around with your head down when you realize what the Word of God says about you. Satan specializes in convincing you that you are missing something. The truth is that you are already blessed!

Everything that I have mentioned is a mindset. We have to change our thinking in order to experience the abundant life that is in Christ. We must adopt a favor paradigm. This means that your underlying thoughts, desires, and actions are influenced by your revelation of God's favor at work in your life. When I caught hold of this revelation of God's favor, it completely transformed my life. I stopped thinking scarcity, and I started thinking abundance. Every day I wake up in the morning, I command the favor of God to work on my behalf. I say, "Lord, I thank You for Your goodness, favor, and wisdom manifesting in every area of my life." I expect preferential treatment and open doors every day. This is the favor paradigm. The Bible says in Philippians 4:8:

> *Finally, brethren, whatsoever things are true, whatsoever things are honest, whatsoever things are just, whatsoever things are pure, whatsoever things are lovely, whatsoever things are of good report; if there be any virtue, and if there be any praise, think on these things.*

The Bible instructs us to only think on things that are true, honest, just, pure, lovely, virtuous, and praiseworthy. This way of thinking requires practice. We have to train our mind to meditate on the Word of God at all times, no matter what. The Bible does not say that we are to think on good things because good things happen, but we are to make a deliberate decision to think on these things as an act of our faith. The more you think on good things, the more good things happen. Do not subscribe to negativity just because negative circumstances arise; declare the Word of God over your circumstances. Declare, "The Favor of God surrounds me as a shield."

The challenge we have is that this way of thinking does not come natural to us. Most of us were taught to be negative the vast majority of our lives. This is why Word mediation is crucial if you want to change your thinking. Whatever area you find your thinking the most negative, that is the area that you need to apply God's Word the most. I dare you to allow the Word of God to shift your paradigm. I dare you to think abundance instead of lack. The moment you do this, you will experience a change. It may be a small change, but it will be a change nonetheless; and before you know it, you will no longer identify with that old way of thinking.

HIS FAVOR IS SUFFICIENT

*And he said unto me, **My grace** [favor] **is sufficient for thee**: for my strength is made perfect in weakness. Most gladly therefore will I rather glory in my infirmities, that the power of Christ may rest upon me* (2 Corinthians 12:9).

Apostle Paul was definitely no stranger to challenges. Prior to his vocation as a preacher and teacher of the Gospel, he made a living by persecuting the church and facilitating the murder of Christians. After God arrested him and changed his name (and his calling), Paul became one of the most influential figures in Christianity. As a matter of fact, he wrote 80 percent of what we now know as the New Testament.

During his tenure ministering to the Gentiles, Paul experienced much persecution from both Jewish believers and non-Jewish believers alike. He often had to press through slander, false accusation, and Judaizers, just to name a few. In the book of Second Corinthians,

Paul came to a place where he could not take it anymore. He cried out to God and asked Him to remove the "thorn in the flesh," which by the way had nothing to do with sickness. Paul cried out three times and asked God to remove the affliction he was experiencing. To this request, God responded, "My favor (grace) is sufficient." Why would God respond in such a way? He tells us exactly why He responds this way in the next part of the verse, "for my strength is made perfect in weakness."

Earlier I introduced the concept of the favor paradigm and the supernatural shift necessary in order to accommodate this way of thinking. The truth is that the favor of God is not just for the good times—it is necessary the most in times of weakness. When we think of favor, we think of preferential treatment and blessing; it is definitely that, but it is also so much more. God told Paul that it was not a matter of Him removing the affliction, but in fact, His favor was all that was necessary to endure the hardship. Remember, we are not just speaking of any kind of favor, we are talking about supernatural favor. This is the supernatural power made available by God to deal with any issue in our lives. This supernatural favor is all that we need.

So many Christians find themselves in a state of anguish when faced with a difficult situation. We look to God to deliver us, when in fact the favor of God has already been poured out, and that favor has all that you need. It is not a matter of God rescuing you from the pain or difficulty, it is a matter of adopting the favor paradigm. I have been in countless circumstances where I just knew that it was over. I would threaten God by telling Him that I couldn't take it anymore. God wouldn't say a word. After I was finished pouting, the voice of the Lord would come to me, "Son, I have already given you everything that you need to overcome this situation." Essentially, God was telling me that His grace was sufficient.

> *We look to God to deliver us, when in fact the favor of God has already been poured out, and that favor has all that you need.*

Let us examine that word for a moment: sufficient. This is the Greek word *arkeo* (Strong's, G714), and it means to be possessed of unfailing strength, to be strong. God never told Paul that He would not remove the difficulty, He simply said that His favor was packed with enough unfailing strength to deal with what he was facing. Once we as believers really come into the understanding that the favor of God is more powerful than anything that we are facing right now, we will approach life from an entirely different vantage point. So instead of worrying, fretting, and complaining, open your mouth and declare, "God's favor is sufficient for me. His strength is made perfect in my weakness!"

There is no need to be moved out of a position of faith and expectation, because the favor of God is strong enough to open the door, bring the increase, manifest the blessing, and whatever else is necessary. Paul decided to stop complaining and boast in his struggles, because he adopted the favor paradigm. This paradigm enables you to identify the goodness and favor of God in any situation you find yourself. You will always have something to be grateful for. The more you do this, the more the Bible says the power of Christ will begin to rest on you. This is the key. Make up in your mind that the favor

God has already given you is more than enough, and watch the supernatural power of Christ manifest in your circumstances.

FAVOR DECLARATION

Father, in the name of Jesus, I thank You for who You are and all that You have done in my life. I come to You with a grateful heart. Today I declare and confess in the name of Jesus Christ that I have joy unspeakable and am full of glory. I declare that the joy of the Lord is my strength. I walk in righteousness, peace, and joy in the Holy Ghost. I am not moved by circumstances in my life, but I have decided to rejoice. I rejoice in You always. Today is the day of joy. I am excited about Your goodness in my life today. My joyful attitude is contagious. Others will look at me today and ask me the very source of my joy. Thank You, Lord Jesus, for making my cup run over. I am overflowing with joy and thanksgiving right now, in Jesus' name. Amen!

Chapter 12

IT'S ALREADY YOURS

And of his fulness have all we received,
and grace for grace (John 1:16).

I<small>N ALL THAT WE HAVE EXAMINED UP TO THIS POINT, THE MOST</small> powerful truth of all is that the favor of God is already yours. There is nothing that you and I can do to earn God's favor. His favor is simply a display of His unconditional love for us. God so loved the world (according to John 3:16) that He gave His only begotten Son, that whoever believes in Him should not perish, but have everlasting life. This is the entire basis of the Gospel of the kingdom of God; the underserving love and compassion the Father has displayed in Christ.

We have a tendency to forget this truth when we are going about our daily lives. We somehow believe that there is something apart from God that has the capacity to meet our needs, but the truth is—there is nothing else. God has already done His part, you and I simply need to enter into this reality by faith. The supernatural favor of God is a kingdom reality! The favor of God is a covenant right. It was given to us the moment we became born again. Why? Because when we became born again, we entered into a covenant relationship with God. Remember, God is a covenant God! The question is: how do you and I partake of this favor that was already given to us?

The Bible says in the Gospel of John chapter 1 verse 16, "And of his fulness have all we received, and grace for grace." What does Apostle John mean when he says that we have received of His fullness? He is speaking of Jesus Christ Himself, and he is saying that we have already received His fullness. The word fullness here is the Greek word *pleroma* (Strong's, G4138), and it literally means a full ship. The Bible is telling us that when Jesus came to the earth realm, He was loaded with the favor, power, and anointing of God. The moment we accepted Him by faith (as the expression goes), our ship came in!

Where I live in Tampa, Florida, we have huge cargo ships that come into the Port of Tampa from the Gulf of Mexico. These ships are loaded with all sorts of goods and materials ready to be unloaded and transported. Like these ships, Jesus Christ sailed from the loading station of heaven into the port of earth, and He was packed to capacity. What was He loaded with? He was loaded with the favor of Almighty God. This is what the Bible is referring to when it uses the phrase "grace for grace." Christ came to bring the grace of God in abundance. As a matter of fact, the Bible says that the law came by Moses, but grace and truth came by Jesus Christ. Jesus was the captain of the cargo ship called grace, and this ship is full.

What does it mean to receive? This is one of the most important principles in the Bible. The Greek word for receive in John 1:16 is the word *lambano* (Strong's, G2983), and it means to "take a thing due." This implies that one has the right to possess something. To receive something, we must lay hold of it by faith. Before we can receive this supernatural favor, we have to believe that we have a right to it. As I mentioned before, this favor is not simply an added benefit to the Christian life—it is part of the redemption package. The key is being convinced that it already belongs to you. Once you believe something already belongs to you, you will be in a position of confidence and expectation. If you were to go to the grocery store and buy produce, you wouldn't ask the clerk if you could walk out with the items you just purchased; no, you would confidently expect them to place your items in a bag and thank you for shopping. Why don't we expect the favor of God to manifest in our lives every day?

> *Before we can receive this supernatural favor,*
> *we have to believe that we have a right to it.*

A LESSON IN RECEIVING

Let me tell you about one my wife's stories of supernatural favor. Gloria was in her final year of college and was eager like most of the college seniors to get an internship and secure employment before graduation. Every year at her school a big career fair would be held to connect the students with potential employers. So she prepared for her opportunity to meet employers and hopefully secure an internship. The market was highly competitive and she was a little nervous.

The day finally came and she put on her brand-new suit, grabbed her new briefcase, prepared an awesome résumé, and arrived at school four hours before the fair. As she walked to the fair she prayed, and she heard the Lord speak to her audibly, telling her what company she would work for. There were more than fifteen potential employers at the fair. After she walked around and handed out résumés to all the different employers, the final table she encountered on her way out was the company she heard God tell her about. As she was approaching the table, a man walked out in front of her and immediately said, "I want you to come and work for us." He selected her out of the hundreds of students who had come to his table that day.

Before he saw her impressive résumé or had a chance to speak to her, God's favor set her apart. Three interviews later, she was offered a position at this company and went on to work for them. The interviews were scary and did not go so well, but God reminded her, "It's already yours." Even before she went to the career fair, God already gave the job to her. This is an example of how the favor of God works in our lives.

Many of us are asking God to bless us, heal us, deliver us, and prosper us, when in reality He has already done that. All you and I need to do is receive it. The ship of favor is loaded with more than you and I can even imagine. We don't have to strive, manipulate, or struggle to experience the blessings of God in our lives; all we need to do is believe that God has already done it. As a minister, it breaks my heart to see so many people living beneath their potential. God has more for us than we often realize.

I share my wife's story to prove that there is no circumstance or situation that exists in which God will not display His favor and loving-kindness toward us. I believe that God wanted her to know that He loved her and that He was concerned about her. He is concerned about everything in our lives. I want to tell you that God loves you more than you realize. Do not allow the enemy to discourage you or convince you that your life is supposed to be filled with struggle. God wants you to enjoy your life. He wants you to experience His goodness, favor, wisdom, and compassion every day you wake up.

> *Do not allow the enemy to discourage you or convince you that your life is supposed to be filled with struggle. God wants you to enjoy your life.*

The questions remain: Are you convinced that it already belongs to you? Do you believe that it is your right to walk in the supernatural favor of God? *Whatever you are convinced about will become the force that dominates your life.* You have to learn to use your expectation to draw from the unlimited fountain of God's supernatural favor.

REIGNING IN LIFE

*For if by one man's offence death reigned by one; much more they which receive abundance of grace and of the gift of righteousness shall **reign in life** by one, Jesus Christ* (Romans 5:17).

The simple yet profound truth is that God wants us to reign in life. I heard this concept preached for years, but I never really had a clue what it meant. What does it mean to reign in life? Well, the Bible tells us in Romans chapter 5 verse 17, that you and I are supposed to reign. The literal translation of this word in the Greek is to exercise kingly power. The hallmark of any king is dominion. God wants us to dominate situations, circumstances, and difficulties (not people) in our lives like kings. I know this concept seems a bit far off to us, because we have been taught to embrace defeat. We have been coerced by religion into being victims of the things that happen to us.

Beloved, God does not want you to live that way. He wants you to walk in the blessing of Abraham. Abraham reigned in life. As a matter of fact, Abraham had so much authority and dominion in the earth that he and his servants defeated kings. When was the last time you took the members of your household and fought a war? Now that is what I call supernatural favor! The beauty is that this same favor is available to us. There are some battles that you and I face every day and we need to be equipped with more than just our emotions.

In context, Romans 5:17 is talking about the fall of Adam. Through Adam's transgression, death reigned from Adam to Moses and so on. Contrariwise, through the righteous obedience of Christ, grace (or favor) has been manifested in the lives of those of us who believe. Furthermore, you and I have been given the gift of righteousness. This is a very important aspect to the supernatural favor of God, because without righteousness we cannot stand in God's presence confidently. I think it is important to stress the fact that righteousness implies right standing as well as right living. We must live a lifestyle pleasing to God if we want to experience His favor; however, we are only able to live this way because of what Jesus accomplished on the cross. Most people don't see the divine connection between Christ's finished work on the cross and the manifestation of divine favor in their daily lives. This connection is a very real part of the new life.

Now that we have established the truth that you and I have been made righteous in Christ, the second dimension to our ability to reign in life is the grace of God. The Bible says that we must receive the "abundance of grace." The word receive is the same Greek word *(lambano)* that we discussed previously. The more you and I lay hold of God's favor by faith and expectation, the more we will see that favor manifested, and the more we will reign in life. This Scripture literally transformed my life. There is a "force field of goodness" that surrounds you right now! This force field keeps the blessings of God in and the cares of this life out.

After the fall of man, the human race became ruled by the circumstances of life. This was part of the curse. God told Adam that he would toil all the days of his life. This is how most Christians live to this day; they toil for everything that they need in life. This ought not to be! God wants us to live in His abundance and take dominion in the earth. We do this by taking hold of the abundance of God's grace. Favor is a force, and the more we come into alignment with this favor, the more the atmosphere of our lives will shift.

> *Favor is a force, and the more we come*
> *into alignment with this favor, the more*
> *the atmosphere of our lives will shift.*

This favor is tangible. People can sense it operating in your life; they can even see it on you! The more evident this favor is, the more people feel compelled to bless you and prefer you. One day I was in a restaurant ministering to a friend of mine. When we approached the register, an older lady came up to me and said that she overheard our conversation and she never heard the Gospel presented in such a way. She insisted that I should allow her to pay for my meal. Since I could tell that she was sincere, I kindly obliged. Hallelujah to the Lamb! I want to live in that kind of favor every day. This is not luck, it's supernatural favor. The more of this favor you receive, the more circumstances and situations will bow before you.

FAVOR DECLARATION

Father, in the name of Jesus, I thank You for who You are and all that You have done. Right now I decree and declare that I have perfect fellowship with You. I reign in every area of my life. In accordance with Romans 5:17, I have the gift of righteousness and I take dominion over situations, circumstances, and resources. I receive divine answers to my prayers. I love to pray and spend time with You, Father. I receive (by faith) the abundant blessings that You have already given me in Christ. I exercise kingly power as an ambassador of Jesus Christ and the kingdom of God. I am absolutely convinced that I have a right to walk in Your supernatural favor and this favor dominates my life. Thank You, Lord, that Your promises are already mine. In Jesus' name. Amen!

Chapter 13

No More Lack

A land wherein thou shalt eat bread without
scarceness, thou shalt not lack any thing in it;
a land whose stones are iron, and out of whose
hills thou mayest dig brass (Deuteronomy 8:9).

I DON'T KNOW ABOUT YOU, BUT I HAVE SEEN SOME VERY DARK DAYS in my life. There was a time when I thought I would never experience God's abundance in my life. I was tempted during those times to do what most people do—give up.

Did you know that most people suffer from something called cognitive dissonance? What is that? It is a psychological term that refers to a state of inconsistent thoughts, attitudes, and beliefs; especially as it relates to our behavior. This takes place when what we say we believe doesn't match our current reality. However, this concept goes much deeper.

Years ago I heard a story about a fox and sour grapes. One day this fox saw a patch of grapes across a fence. Having his heart set on eating the grapes, the fox traveled under the fence to retrieve his prize. Unfortunately, the fox underestimated the height of this grape patch, and when he came close to the patch, he realized that it was too high for him to reach. After attempting to jump and reach the patch of grapes time and time again, he finally convinced himself that his attempts were futile. As the fox finally gave up and walked away he said, "I didn't want those sour grapes anyway!"

This illustration speaks to the state of many in the church. In their frustration with the circumstances of their lives, they convince themselves that things will never change. They even go as far as to despise the blessings that God intends for them to have. They tell themselves that they don't want that particular blessing or promotion anymore. Beloved, I am here to tell you that this is a trick of the evil one. As a matter of fact, that is one of the main reasons why I wrote this book: to give you hope that there is a much better life available to you. Many people have come to accept lack and insufficiency as a normal way of life. They go to church and sing songs of praise, but inwardly they are frustrated and angry at the dissonance between what they are saying out of their mouths and what they are actually experiencing.

I have definitely been in this situation. In fact, I used to be just like the fox in the story. I can remember a time when I would lead worship on Sunday morning and come home to an apartment that had no electricity. I would tell other people that God was *Jehovah Jireh* (Strong's, H3070) (The One Who Provides) while all of my bills were past due. I was so angry inside that I didn't know what to do. The irony of all of this is the fact that I gave tithes regularly. My first reaction was to blame my circumstances. I even went as far as to attack ministries and preachers who taught prosperity. I said that they were false preachers. In my mind, the grapes (favor, blessings, and prosperity of God) where simply sour. The truth was my approach was wrong.

> *God was trying to teach me for years how to experience His abundance, but I was rejecting His wisdom and instruction.*

Many people are too prideful to admit that they are wrong. Instead of changing their approach, they simply come up with a philosophy to justify their position in life. The Bible tells us in Deuteronomy 8:9 that we will "eat bread without scarceness." What does this mean? This is the Hebrew word *mickenuth* (Strong's, H4544), and it literally means poverty. God does not want you to be in poverty. The Word of God teaches us that poverty or scarcity is a curse. The Bible says, "thou shalt not lack anything…." This is good news! When God said in His Word that we shall lack nothing, He meant exactly what He said. So what is the disconnect? If God says that we shall lack nothing, why are there so many people who seem to lack so much? I have said before that whatever we are convicted about will become the force that dominates our lives. If you accept lack, then lack will become a force that dominates your life.

We know, biblically, that favor is a supernatural force that attracts blessing, provision, and divine prosperity. When we align ourselves with this force called favor, it begins to produce tremendous results in our lives. On the other hand, if we (like that little fox) despise the favor of God, we will push it away from us. God was trying to teach me for years how to experience His abundance, but I was rejecting His wisdom and instruction. Then one day God began to unveil to me this very revelation that I am sharing with you. My life took a dramatic turn.

THE LAW OF CHEERFULNESS

There are spiritual laws that govern the kingdom of God. Ignorance of these laws can be detrimental to our spiritual, physical, and emotional well-being. The Bible says in Hosea chapter 4, verse 6 that "My people are destroyed for lack of knowledge." Many Christians believe that they can ignore these laws and still live a successful and prosperous life. This is a serious mistake.

By law I am not referring to the Ten Commandments specifically, but I am talking more about spiritual principles that God has established in His Word that govern our ability to enjoy all of the benefits and blessings that He has for us. For instance, the law of gravity. If we respect the law of gravity, we will live wonderful lives; but if we disregard this law, we may find ourselves in a very hazardous predicament. In the same manner, many Christians are struggling because they refuse to obey the laws of God. Here I was, a Spirit-filled tither who was in a constant state of financial lack. What was the problem? I thought God said that if I paid my tithes, I would be blessed. Though that is a true statement, it is not a complete statement. Now I do want to strongly emphasize the importance of tithing and giving our offering to the Lord. Recent studies show that less than 10% of people who profess Christianity in America, give tithes and offerings faithfully to God. This is a very disturbing statistic. You can imagine why there are so many people who are not experiencing the blessings of God in their lives, because they are refusing to conform to His plan for their finances. Remember... tithing is an expression of our love and submission to God. Simply stated, tithing is an act of our worship.

When you see giving this way, it changes the dynamics how you approach giving forever. God is not just looking at the amount of our giving, He is looking at the attitude of our hearts while we are giving—just like God is concerned with our hearts with any expression of worship. Imagine going to church and singing songs of worship to the Lord and you hate the person sitting next to you. Your worship is not acceptable to God! Why? Because of the condition of your heart. This is why God tells us to forgive. He wants us to approach Him with a pure conscious and a pure heart.

The same goes for our finances. God is not just interested in your money. He is after so much more! Second Corinthians chapter 9 explains this concept. It says that when we sow into God's kingdom (when we give our money), we are not to do it grudgingly or of necessity, because "the Lord loves a cheerful giver." This is what I call the law of cheerfulness. This law governs our capacity to experience God's abundance in our lives. All those years that I was giving to the church, I did it with anger and frustration in my heart. I was upset at the circumstances in my life and the prolonged season of lack. I was approaching God with a sense of entitlement.

Entitlement is not the same as expectation. One of them is rooted in doubt and pride, while the other is motivated by faith and expectation. This is very important to understand. The word that is used for cheerful in Second Corinthians is literally the word hilarious. When something is hilarious, it makes you laugh; it produces a sense of joy. This is how we are supposed to approach every opportunity to give to God. We ought to be excited that God would allow us to worship Him with our finances.

Many people do the exact opposite of this. Rather than approach God with joy, happiness, and excitement; they choose to give grudgingly. What does it mean to give grudgingly? It literally means to give out of pain, sorrow, grief, and affliction. Wow! That does not sound too good does it? How do people do this? It's really quite simple! They choose to focus on what they don't have, how much of a sacrifice it is for them to give, and what they are missing out on by giving to God. Most people don't express this verbally, but it takes place in their hearts.

Have you ever said to yourself, *If I give this, then I won't have enough to pay my bills.* This statement violates the law of cheerfulness. There is no way that you can give joyfully while still being obsessed with your circumstances. As a result of violating this aspect of the law of cheerfulness, people actually block their ability to reap a harvest from their sowing.

The other dimension to this principle is the aspect of necessity. The Bible says that we are not to give out of necessity! The word necessity here is the Greek word *anagke* (Strong's, G318) and it means by law of duty, distress, or desperation. We are not supposed to give simply because we have to or out of need. We are to give because we love God. There is a very dangerous teaching in the church today that seeks to manipulate people into giving through guilt and condemnation. *This is not biblical!* God does not want the sacrifice of someone who does not have a covenant relationship with Him. We are to give out of covenant relationship; and when we do, God will always respond bountifully. The moment I caught hold of this truth, things began to turn around. God began to bless me from every angle. Why? Because I cooperated with a spiritual law. The more you monitor the condition of your heart while you are giving, the easier it will be to develop a habit of giving cheerfully.

> *We are to give out of covenant relationship; and when we do, God will always respond bountifully.*

THE LAW OF HONOR

Honor the Lord with thy substance and with the first-fruits of all thine increase: so shall thy barns be filled with plenty and thy presses shall burst out with new wine (Proverbs 3:9-10).

One of the most important aspects of kingdom living is a scarcely regarded concept called honor. Few people do it and even fewer are aware of its benefits. What is honor? More importantly, what does honor have to do with favor? The word honor comes from the Hebrew word *kabad* (Strong's, H3513), and it means to be heavy or weighty. Honor is an attitude of respect, reverence, and value that we place on someone or something. This simply means that we are to attach value or weight to God. It is kind of like a CEO in a boardroom. When the CEO speaks, the words have weight and value. God is the Chief Executive of the Universe, and we are to attach significance and value to Him in all that we do.

The Bible tells us to honor the Lord with our substance. How do we honor the Lord with our substance? We honor the Lord with our substance by acknowledging Him with our material possessions and in all of our financial decisions. This includes a consistent practice of sowing into God's Kingdom, knowing that by doing so, you are advancing His purpose in the earth. When you sow into the Kingdom of God in faith and expectation, you are posturing yourself to reap a supernatural harvest.

> *We honor the Lord with our substance by acknowledging Him with our material possessions and in all of our financial decisions.*

Let us spend a little more time highlighting the concept of honor. When we honor someone, we esteem that person highly. God should be at the very forefront of our minds when it comes to our giving. After receiving a financial blessing of any kind, is giving to God the first thing on your mind? This is what I call the Law of Honor. This simply means that what you honor, you will respect; and what you respect, you will attract. The more you and I learn to honor God in the various areas of our lives, the more we will attract His favor and goodness.

The Bible says in Ephesians 6:2-3, "Honor thy father and mother...that it may be well with thee." Honoring our parents in the natural realm creates a canapé of blessing and favor that will cover us all the days of our lives. Why? Because God loves honor. This is a dynamic of God's kingdom. He is King and He deserves our honor and respect. When we worship God we are honoring Him, and He always responds to honor.

On the other hand, what you dishonor you will repel. Have you ever given someone a gift and they weren't appreciative? Have you ever seen a child be rude or disrespectful? People who do this are what I call ill-favored. They wonder why things don't work well for them. They speak negatively of their employer, their pastors, and other leaders, and they are frustrated that they have never been promoted or received a salary increase. This is an irrefutable law of the kingdom of God. Whatever you want to attract to your life, you must first learn to respect. If you want to attract God's provision, you must respect God's provision. If you want to attract favor and increase, you must make a decision to honor the Lord.

This is what the Bible promises when we honor the Lord with our substance, "So shall thy barns be filled with plenty and thy presses shall burst out with new wine." This sounds like a promise that I wouldn't mind receiving. The Bible didn't just say that you would be slightly blessed, it says that this blessing will be bursting out. The word for burst out is the Hebrew word *parats* (Strong's, H6555), and it literally means breakthrough. Wow! The breakthrough that you have been looking for is one act of honor away. However, this promise is conditional. It is contingent upon us honoring God in two areas: with our substance and the first fruits of our increase.

We spoke a little about honoring God with our substance earlier. The other area that we are to honor the Lord is with our first fruits. Remember, when we honor someone we give them the right of first choice. Whenever you have a major event taking place in your life, you usually communicate first with the people you honor the most. To dishonor someone means to put them last in all of your decisions. In the same way, to honor God means to put Him first in your life and particularly in your finances. He has the first choice among all of your possessions. This is called first fruits.

God told the children of Israel that the first male who came from the womb belonged to Him. This goes for everything that you have. The blessing of this is that God will cause your barns to be filled with plenty. Your barns represent your bank account. Do you want your bank account full of plenty? Make the sacrifice of honoring God with what already belongs to Him and watch the favor of God manifest in a mighty way.

FAVOR DECLARATION

Father, in the name of Jesus, I thank You for who You are and all that You have done. Today I declare that any and all curses of lack and poverty are broken over my life and mind. Every negative word spoken over me, consciously or unconsciously, is nullified in the name of Jesus Christ. I cancel negative words that I have spoken over myself (or finances) and believed. I am blessed in the name of Jesus, and my heritage is a goodly heritage (Psalm 16:6). I speak crop failure to every word of defeat, failure, destruction, calamity, delay, regression, lack, worry, and unfruitfulness. I declare that everything in my life is working toward my good. I am blessed to be a blessing. In the name of Jesus Christ. Amen!

Chapter 14

An Abundant Supply

But my God shall supply all your need according to
His riches in glory by Christ Jesus (Philippians 4:19).

Y OU ALREADY KNOW BY NOW THAT GOD WANTS TO POUR OUT
His goodness, favor, provision, and blessing in your life like you
have never imagined possible. There is no limit to how far God will
go to show you just how good He really is. I think that many Christians subconsciously believe that God does not have enough blessing
to go around. Maybe they believe that they do not qualify to receive

God's abundance in their lives. Neither one of these beliefs are correct based on the Word of God.

We have examined the truth of the Bible concerning supernatural favor. We have seen that it is our birthright and covenant blessing to walk in the favor of God all of the days of our lives. We have also seen that there are things that we can do to release this favor in our lives; primarily, we must have faith in the promises of God. The Bible tells us that God will supply all of our need. He did not say *some* of our need; He said *all* of our need. Usually when we read that, we automatically assume that God is just referring to our daily necessities such as food, clothing, and shelter, but I believe that God is referring to so much more. In the original Greek the word need also means duty or business. In other words, God is like a venture capitalist; He has a responsibility to fund a business that He owns and controls. We are God's business and whatever our "business" needs to function and to thrive, God promises to supply.

In previous chapters we discussed the truth that God is El Shaddai (The Many Breasted One). God is "The All-Sufficient Source" of more than enough. Whatever we need, He must supply. How does God determine what our needs are? He determines needs based on His Word, not based on our emotions or the gravity of our circumstances. Whatever the Word of God promises us is a need. God promises to supply everything that is needful at any given time based on His purpose and plan for our lives. For example, if you are a pastor and God wants you to expand your church, this is a need as far as God is concerned—and He will supply!

This is awesome news! God says that He will supply everything His Word promises us "according to His riches in glory." What does this mean? This means that God is not limited by our physical limitations. God funds our needs from heaven's unlimited reserves. As simple as this truth is, some of us just don't seem to get it. God is not affected by recessions or "fiscal cliffs"; He draws our supernatural provision from the invisible realm of glory. The word riches in this passage means exactly that—God is wealthy! In fact the Bible says that He owns all the silver and gold (see Haggai 2:8). The Bible also says that God owns the cattle upon a thousand hills (see Psalm 50:10) A thousand hills is a Jewish idiom meaning that God owns everything.

> *When we approach God, we should always have an attitude of faith and expectation because we know that He is full of an abundant supply of favor and blessings.*

Do you realize that God owns everything? Do you actually believe that God has more than enough resources to meet your every need? The Bible means exactly what it says! When we approach God, we should always have an attitude of faith and expectation because we know that He is full of an abundant supply of favor and blessings. The Word of God says that He is able to make *all grace* abound toward you, that you, *always* having *all* sufficiency in *all* things, may have an *abundance* for every good work (see 2 Corinthians 9:8). The word all appears in this passage three times; I think God really wants us to get the point. When you look up the word all sufficiency it literally means a perfect condition of life in which no aid or support is needed. God does not want us to live in a state of constant lack. He wants us to be so full of His goodness that we are able to bless others with what we have.

You may be thinking, *But I don't have more than enough, I'm struggling in my finances.* Remember, you and I have to change the way we think about our finances. Stop limiting yourself to what you see in the natural and make the Word of God your final authority. Don't rehearse the lack in your life; speak abundance. Begin to thank God right now for supplying your every need according to His riches, not yours.

Create a folder in your house called the Abundant Supply folder, and whenever you have a financial need, write it down and place it in this folder. This will help you to reorient your thinking. Imagine that you were the son or daughter of the wealthiest person in the world. Would you ever be afraid that you would go without? Absolutely not! Why? Because you would know that all you have to do is call upon your father. Well, guess what? You *are* the son or daughter of the wealthiest person in the universe; you are a child of the Most High God. Call on His name! Take Him at His Word, and see if you will not experience a breakthrough.

THE LORD IS *YOUR* SHEPHERD

The Bible tells us in Psalm 23, "The Lord is my shepherd, I shall not want." This is one of the most powerful statements in the Bible. The question is: what does it mean? When the writer of the 23rd Psalm said that the Lord was his Shepherd, he was referring to the word *rajah,* which means ruler or guide. Shepherds were very common in ancient Israel. There were so many shepherds that the sheep had to become acclimated to the voice of their shepherd. Usually the shepherd would blow a whistle and this would produce a unique sound that only his flock could discern. Jesus said, "My sheep hear my voice, and a stranger they will not follow." David said that the voice he chose to respond to was the voice of the Lord. To put it another way, he only regarded the Word of God.

You and I have to make a decision to only respond to the Word of God, and to refuse to take heed to any other voice. This is what it means to be shepherded by God; it means that He is the one who leads, guides, and controls our lives.

The second part of this profound promise is that we shall not want. This is an absolute statement. What does this mean? The word want in that passage simply means lack. God says that we will lack nothing. Why? Because the Lord is our Shepherd. He is the one responsible for feeding us and providing for us in every area of our lives. Just as physical shepherds have to protect and provide for their sheep at all times, God is our Shepherd 24 hours a day, 7 days a week. The Word of God promises us that we shall not lack. You have to believe this promise within the deep reservoir of your heart.

> *The Word of God promises us that we shall not lack. You have to believe this promise within the deep reservoir of your heart.*

How can there be so many believers who live in a state of lack when the Bible clearly says that we shall not lack? It is because they are not following the guide of the Good Shepherd. Instead they are listening to the voice of a "stranger." By stranger, I am referring to any other influence contrary to the Word of God. There must be an overwhelming confidence that God is our Shepherd. Our ability to enjoy any promise in God's Word must be based on faith. I am not referring to religious jargon or emotionalism; I am talking about being convinced in our hearts that the Word is absolutely truth.

There are two kinds of truth—absolute and relative. Relative truth varies depending on situations and circumstances, but absolute truth is a fixed reality. However, you and I have to make up in our minds that the Word of God is absolute truth. The truth is that "you shall not want" (lack). The reason why you shall not lack is because He does not lack; and if you are following His lead, you will experience His abundant supernatural provision. The Bible tells us to take no thought for our lives, we are not to worry about our lives (see Matthew 6:25). How could we possibly not think about our needs when they are so prevalent? Why would God tell us to do that? He is trying to get us to see that He is the one responsible for the needs in our lives.

The world system has taught us that we are supposed to worry about everything. It is as if there is some sort of nobility in grinding our teeth and pulling out our hair when it comes to our problems. The Bible says that we are to cast our cares (worries) on Him (see 1 Peter 5:7). How do we do this? The word cast in the Greek is the word *epiripto* (Strong's, G1977), and it means to literally throw something off of you onto someone else. The word picture is that of a hiker throwing off his backpack so that his partner can carry it. This is what God wants us to do. He wants us to throw off the heavy load of worry and anxiety and give it to Him. Why? Because He cares for us, or as it is expressed in the original Greek, "He does the caring for us." We don't have to worry about anything because God has taken upon Him the task of worrying for us.

Did you know that worrying is a sin? In fact, to worry means that you are literally worshiping your circumstances, and God tells us to put no other god's before Him. Whenever we worry we are telling God that our problems are much bigger than Him. You probably never thought about it this way. Besides, worrying does not help us at all. The Bible says in Matthew 6:27, "Which of you by taking thought can add one cubit unto his stature?" Worry is disempowering, but casting our care on God lightens the load so that we are able to praise and thank Him. The key to experiencing supernatural favor is to constantly acknowledge the goodness of God in every circumstance. Resolve in your heart and mind that you will never worry again. The Lord is your Shepherd!

SUPERNATURAL MULTIPLICATION

I want to share a testimony of God's supernatural abundance being manifested in our lives. One year for our New Year's Eve service we were believing God to bring as many people as possible. Prior to this time we only saw about 40 people during our Sunday services. We began to pray for His increase. In preparation for the New Year, we printed about 150 flyers and distributed them at the local mall in our area. In addition to that, we bought some finger food including some chicken and sandwiches. The day before our event, I kept sensing that we were going to experience God's supernatural power.

The evening of the New Year's Eve service there were more people present than we ever anticipated. None of the people who attended received the flyers that we distributed, they were simply drawn by the Spirit of God. As we were about to close the service, my wife realized that we had a serious problem, there was not enough food to feed everyone. As a matter of fact, it was only enough food to feed our staff and a few more people. My wife prayed over the food. To our amazement, people kept coming back for more and more food. Everyone ate second and third portions. We actually had enough food left over to last us for a whole week.

How was this possible? The food actually multiplied! The more people ate, the more food materialized. Hallelujah! This is what is meant by the term abundant supply. God is the God of more than enough. He brought an abundance of people (more people than we had ever seen in a single service) and an abundance of food to feed those people. We must always realize that the kingdom of God brings increase. In fact, increase is a dynamic of God's kingdom. The more we are conscious of the kingdom, the more increase we will experience.

God wants you and me to experience this supernatural multiplication in every area of our lives. When the favor of God touches what you have, it will multiply. The favor of God is an accelerator and a multiplier. I dare you to put God to the test! We have seen God do things like this time and time again. He loves to demonstrate His favor and goodness. The whole purpose of this book is to encourage you to consider that there is an entire realm in God that you have yet to explore. If God created the universe and spoke the world into being, surely He can supply your every need. Do you believe that God can do everything? If not, dare to believe. Not only can God do everything, but He has *already done* everything. It is time for you to place a real demand on His favor. I don't care what it is that you are faced with today—there is an abundant supply to overcome every obstacle!

FAVOR DECLARATION

Father, in the name of Jesus, I thank You for who You are and all that You have done. Today I declare in the name of Jesus Christ that I am stress free. Worry and anxiety do not have permission to occupy my mind. I cast all of my cares and concerns on Jesus Christ for He cares for me (see 1 Peter 5:7). I am worry free and stress free today! I receive Your abundant supply and Your supernatural multiplication in my life right now, in Jesus' name. Amen!

Chapter 15

LIVING IN THE OVERFLOW

*The thief cometh not, but for to steal, and to kill, and to destroy: I am come that they might have life, and that they might have it **more abundantly** (John 10:10).*

ABSOLUTELY LOVE BEING A FATHER, ESPECIALLY BEING THE FATHER of two beautiful daughters. There is just something about my daughters that I find so adorable. They really know how to spoil their father. Particularly my youngest daughter. Whenever I would send her to the kitchen to get me a glass of water, she would hold the glass under the water dispenser too long, and it would spill over. She wasn't quite tall enough at the time to see the level of water in the glass. I guess you would say she allowed the glass to overflow. This is exactly how God wants us to live. He wants us to experience the overflow of His good favor.

In the Gospel of John chapter 10, the Bible tells us that Jesus came so we could have life and have it more abundantly. It seems redundant for the writer of John's Gospel to use the phrase "more abundantly." I promise you that this is not an accident or a mistranslation. This is the exact thought that heaven intended to convey to the born-again believer. The phrase more abundantly there is the Greek word *perissos* (Strong's, G4053), and it means exceeding some number or measure, over and above, more than necessary, and superadded. Wow! That is quite an expression! This is the life that Jesus came to give us. He wants us to be abounding with His joy until it is full to overflowing. Like the glass in my daughter's hand, our lives should be running over with the blessings of God.

Satan is the thief. He wants to kill, steal, and destroy. He wants you to suffer, lack, defeat, depression, and despair. None of those things are from God. Our heavenly Father wants us blessed. In fact, I believe that Abraham was an example of how God intended His children to live. Abraham lived in the overflow. His life was marked by a deep intimacy with God and an open heaven. Abraham was so blessed that the land could not even contain all of his possessions and all of his relatives (see Genesis 13:6). That is what I call serious abundance.

Let me help you; abundance is not a curse word, neither is prosperity. We know that there are people who abuse the Word of God for selfish gain, but that has nothing to do with you. God wants you blessed. Why? Because He wants to pour out His goodness and compassion through you. We are ambassadors of the Most High God. We are representatives of the kingdom of God. Do you know what that means? It means that we are the physical representation on earth of what heaven is supposed to look like. There is no depression in heaven, so why are so many Christians depressed? There is no poverty in heaven, so why are so many Christians living paycheck to paycheck? There is not a single Scripture that condones that situation.

> *There is no depression in heaven, so why are so many Christians depressed? There is no poverty in heaven, so why are so many Christians living paycheck to paycheck?*

Some may say, "But Christians are supposed to suffer persecution." Those who live godly in Christ will be lied about, talked about, and mistreated—but not by God. This persecution comes by way of the world system, not God. All God wants to do is bless you. Even in His chastisement, it is ultimately to bring you to a place of blessing. It is time for us to stop allowing the enemy to steal from us. The Word of God is very clear. The will of God is that you and I experience life, overflowing to the full.

What does this life look like? In John 10:10, it uses the Greek word *zoe* (Strong's, G2222) to refer to this life. This is actually the same life that is resident in God Himself. So when the Bible says that we are to have life *(zoe)* more abundantly, it is literally saying that

God wants to manifest heaven on the earth. We don't have to wait until we die to experience God's favor and goodness, we can experience the atmosphere and culture of heaven while we are on the earth. Our ultimate reward is in heaven, but God wants us to represent Him correctly while we wait. I have had enough of seeing the enemy rape and pillage God's people. Enough is enough! Jesus came to destroy the works of satan, which includes poverty, lack, and defeat. It is time for us to live in the overflow.

> *We don't have to wait until we die to experience God's favor and goodness, we can experience the atmosphere and culture of heaven while we are on the earth.*

YOU'RE FULL OF IT!

In Ephesians 5:18, the Bible says, "And be not drunk with wine, wherein is excess; but be filled with the Spirit." What does it mean to be filled with the Spirit? This actually comes from the Greek word *pleroo* (Strong's, G4137), and it means to fill to the top. It reminds me of the wedding in Cana in John chapter 2 where Jesus was asked to fix the problem of insufficient wine for the wedding feast. Mary instructed the servants to do whatever Jesus told them to do. In the seventh verse, Jesus told the servants to fill the water pots that were available; the Bible records that they filled them to the brim. Though this is a different word, it essentially has the same meaning as Ephesians 5. We are like the water pots in John 2, and God wants us to be filled to the full with His supernatural favor, power, and love. Once

He fills us, we will be transformed from that which is natural, average, and mundane to that which is supernatural. As a matter of fact, this is exactly what the transformation of water to wine represents; the manifestation of the supernatural favor of God.

In ancient Israel, whenever there was a wedding, the governor of the feast would bring out his best wine to impress and honor his guests. It was a symbol of blessing and prosperity. In this case, the miracle that Jesus performed reserved the best for last. I believe that this is a prophetic sign for the body of Christ. We are living in the last days, and God is pouring out His supernatural favor and prosperity on the church like never before to prepare us for the greatest harvest in human history. Just like those water pots, the favor that is on your life will become satisfaction for everyone around you. This is what it means to live in the overflow.

One of the most selfish things that a believer can do is refuse to prosper. If you don't make up in your mind that you are going to allow God to use you to reach everyone around you and demonstrate His goodness through you, then you are missing out on a tremendous opportunity. Ephesians says that we are not to be drunk with physical wine, but we are to be filled with the Spirit. What does all of this have to do with the favor of God? Simple! The Holy Spirit is the Spirit of Grace. He is the courier of the favor of God. He is the one who moves on the hearts of people to bless you. He is the one who supernaturally opens doors of provision. He is the one who draws blessings and increase to you and me like a magnet.

We are supposed to be full of the Spirit. This is not just a quick douse—this is a deluge. If we are filled with the Spirit then we cannot be simultaneously filled with defeatism and lack. The infilling of God's Spirit is the entrance to this overflowing life of which I speak. In fact, the Bible further expounds in Ephesians 5:19, "Speaking to yourselves in psalms and hymns and spiritual songs, singing and making melody in your heart to the Lord." The word melody is the word *psallo* (Strong's, G5567) and it means to pluck a string or to twang. In other words, when you and I begin to live in the overflow, God will cause our lives to become a song. What song is your life singing right now? Does your life's song testify of the goodness of God, or does it ring of the dissonant cord of despair?

I don't know about you, but I want my life to sing of the goodness of the Lord. It is a choice that you and I have to make. Will we walk in the steps of our father Abraham, or will we follow the example of the world system. God has so much for us! He wants you to know what you have been afforded in Christ. We have a covenant with God that involves the pouring out of His favor on every area of our lives. He wants us to live under an open heaven for the rest of our days on this earth. It is possible! All you have to do is receive it. No more barely getting by! It's time to thrive and walk in superabundance.

Are you ready? Do you want to live in the overflow? You're already full of it!

FAVOR DECLARATION

Father, in the name of Jesus, I thank You for who You are and all that You have done in my life. I declare that today is the day of the Lord's favor. I walk in the favor of God today. I am distinct from the people around me. I walk in grace and preferential treatment. Doors are opened unto me today supernaturally. I am a magnet of divine favor and supernatural blessings. Everywhere I go today, someone will be used by God to do extraordinary things for me. The door of promotion and increase are opened to me today. I will receive both natural and spiritual gifts today. People shall give into my bosom today. All grace abounds toward me in a way that causes me to have all sufficiency in all areas of my life. I will meet someone today that will favor me financially. People are compelled to do wonderful things for me today. In Jesus' name. Amen!

ABOUT KYNAN BRIDGES

AT THE TENDER AGE OF 15, PASTOR KYNAN COMMITTED HIS LIFE to Jesus Christ and was subsequently filled with the Holy Spirit. After getting involved in his local church, God made His call manifest to Kynan audibly. For many years, Kynan served in the local church and was involved with various ministries. After running from the call of God; he was finally arrested by the Holy Spirit. Several years ago, the Lord told Kynan to begin a teaching ministry in Tampa, FL. At this point, the vision for Grace & Peace Global Fellowship was birthed.

> *For if by one man's offense death reigned by one; much more they which receive abundance of grace and of the gift of righteousness shall reign in life by one, Jesus Christ* (Romans 5:17).

This is the vision and mission of Kynan Bridges Ministries: to see the person, power, and presence of Jesus Christ manifested in the lives of people everywhere that they might reign in life. Through his ministry, Pastor Kynan desires to see millions of souls saved and restored through the Gospel of Jesus Christ. He accomplishes this mission by proclaiming the unadulterated, life changing, Word of

God. His outreach ministry serves as the catalyst to spread this message. Every week, he provides resources to people so that they might become more conscious of Christ's love for them and enter into the fullness of His finished work and thereby be positioned to walk in their God ordained assignment, namely the Great Commissioned as outlined in Matthew 28:19.

Pastor Kynan host a weekly podcast (FaithTalk) which serves as a platform to discuss various issues in the body of Christ and the world, and shed light on those issues through the illumination of God's Word. Pastor Kynan and his wife are committed to spreading the gospel through their preaching ministry, speaking engagements, teaching resources, and internet and media platforms. He has been charged with taking the message of the Kingdom of God and its supernatural manifestation to the nations of the earth.

To date, he has reached countless numbers of people with the gospel. Through the combined efforts of his weekly outreach ministry and new media resources, Pastor Kynan has exposed hundreds of thousands to the Gospel of Grace every single week. Currently his outreach efforts are effectively communicating God's Word to people in North America, India, Haiti, and Nigeria. Ultimately, his purpose is to equip the people of God to walk in their supernatural identity and fulfill their Kingdom assignment in the earth.

Pastor Kynan is committed to allowing the power and anointing of the Holy Spirit to flow through him and touch God's people. He is a committed husband, mentor, and father to three beautiful children: Ella, Naomi, and Isaac.